WORLD RELIGIONS SERIES
Series Editor: W. Owen Cole

Hinduism

V.P. (Hemant) Kanitkar

Stanley Thornes & Hulton

First published in 1989 by:
Stanley Thornes (Publishers) Ltd
Old Station Drive
Leckhampton
CHELTENHAM GL53 0DN
England

Typeset by Tech-Set, Gateshead, Tyne & Wear
Printed and bound in Great Britain at The Bath Press, Avon

British Library Cataloguing in Publication Data

Kanitkar, V. P. (Vithal Pralhad), *1927–*
  Hinduism.
  1. Hinduism
  I. Title   II. Series
  294.5

ISBN 1–871402–09–3

Acknowledgements

My sincere thanks are due to my wife, Dr Helen A. Kanitkar, for her constant encouragement and invaluable comments; to Mrs Barbara Nelson-Smith for the meticulous care taken by her in the preparation of the typescript; to Dr W. Owen Cole for his guidance and caring criticism; to Mr Leslie Pringle and to Ms Carrie Mercier for their useful suggestions; to Mr and Mrs Atmaram Jirapuré for permitting Mr Yeshwant Mali to photograph some images in the Shri Sai Temple, 25 Hoop Lane, Golders Green, London NW11; and to Dr R.B. Shah and other members of the managing committee of the Swaminarayan Temple, 46–54 Meadow Garth, London NW10, for their kind hospitality during my visit to the temple.

V.P. (Hemant) Kanitkar

The author and publishers are grateful to the following for permission to reproduce photographs:

Madhukar Amrité, page 25 • Hulton Picture Company (Hulton-Deutsch collection), page 103 • British Museum, reproduced by courtesy of the Trustees of the British Museum, page 62 • W. Owen Cole, page 6 • © the *Daily Telegraph*, page 50 • High Commission of India, page 108 • John Hillelson Agency, © Raghubir Singh, page 22 • Imperial War Museum, page 87 • Robert Jackson, pages 12 (bottom left), 33 (left), 113 and cover (top left) • Yeshwant Mali, pages 49, 52, 78 and 82 • Ann & Bury Peerless, pages 4, 9, 16, 28, 38, 55 (right), 63, 88, 89, 94, 95, 100 and cover (top right) • Popperfoto, page 56 • Shree Prajapati Association UK, pages 12 (top left and right, bottom right), 70 and cover (bottom right) • Sri Aurobindo Society (UK), page 112 • Vrindaban Research Institute, pages 31, 33 (right), 35, 54, 57, 59, 84, 96 and cover (bottom left).

The photographs on pages 10, 14, 34, 41, 45 and 55 (left) were taken by the author.

Every effort has been made to contact copyright holders and we apologise if any have been overlooked.

Contents

Note

These three important words look very similar, but they have very different meanings:

Brahman = the Absolute, God

Brahma = one of the Hindu gods, associated especially with Creation

Brahmin = a member of the priestly caste

Introduction

The vast majority of Indians (about 80 per cent) are Hindus. The word 'Hindu' was used by the ancient Persians to describe the people who lived on the other side of the river Indus, (see map on page vii). Foreigners have always used the word 'Hinduism' to describe the religion of Indians, though Hindus themselves call their religion *Sanatana-dharma*, which means 'ancient religion' or 'eternal rule of life'. *Dharma* means 'religion'; it also means 'a code of moral and religious duty'.

Unlike other major religions, Hinduism has no historical founder, and it has many holy books, not just one. Strictly speaking, it is more than a religion; it is an 'eternal rule of life' and can be followed to a large extent even by non-Hindus. Some Hindus consider all other faiths to be forms of Hinduism, which, as we shall see, influences every aspect of life.

Hindus worship one God, but this 'One God' is worshipped under many names and in many different appearances, both male and female. Yoga and meditation; the Hare Krishna movement; Diwali celebrations at school and at home with lights, joss-sticks, sweetmeats and worship of Laxmi (the Goddess of Wealth and Good Fortune) or Rama (the hero of the Ramayana); all these, and many more, are aspects of the faith that is Hinduism.

Hinduism is an integral part of life and everyday experience for Hindus. To illustrate the extent to which this is true, personal experiences are included here and in Chapter 1. The account below shows the influence of Hinduism in the life of the author.

A Hindu Childhood

I was born in India and lived in a village till I was 11. My village is about 175 miles south-east of Bombay in western India. At that time about 600 people lived there; the majority of men were farmers, each one owning some of the fields which surrounded the village. In the village square was a temple dedicated to a goddess, the guardian deity of the village. Opposite the temple was the only primary school and next to it was the village grocery shop. A river nearby provided water for drinking, washing clothes and bathing. Near the river was a large temple dedicated to Shiva, an important Hindu god, and three houses: two belonged to the priests who performed weddings and funerals for the villagers and the third one belonged to my father, who ran the school. At the far end of the village, away from the village square, lived the leather-workers and the rope-makers.

When I left the village primary school, I went to a high school in a nearby town. As well as Mathematics, Science, Geography and History, including British History, we had to learn four languages. The first one was Marathi, a language spoken widely in western India. The second was Sanskrit, an ancient classical language of India and the language of all Hindu scriptures. We also had to learn Hindi, because it was the national language, and our teacher told us that we would benefit in the long run if we studied English, which was a foreign language introduced by the British when they ruled India.

Studying in London

Soon after 1950, I went to study in London. I had three Indian friends at college. One was from Calcutta and spoke Bengali, the second came from Delhi, the capital of India, and spoke Hindi, the third originated from Madras and spoke Tamil.

The four of us came from four corners of India, spoke different languages and were used to different regional foods. We represented both the variety and the unity of Indians. Once we were invited for a meal by our friend from Madras. After two mouthfuls of rice and curry, I had tears in my eyes. 'Why are you crying?' he asked. 'Are you homesick?' 'No,' I replied. 'You have put too much chilli powder in the curry. It is very hot. I can't eat it.' I ate only rice and natural yoghurt, leaving the curry well alone. My family are vegetarians and we avoid even onion and garlic on certain occasions. I found out that my friends from Delhi and Calcutta occasionally ate meat and fish. There were two things, however, that my friends and I had in common: we all spoke English, which made communication easy and helped us forget our regional differences, and we were all Hindus. Once we went to a newly opened Hindu temple in London to celebrate a festival in honour of a Hindu goddess, which made us very much aware of the second common bond, our religion, Hinduism.

INDIA

Hinduism cannot really be fully understood without knowing something about India, where this great religion started and developed. The different aspects of Hinduism that we see in Britain today are regional variations of practices found in India.

From the map you can see that India is separated from the rest of Asia by an arc of very high mountains. These are the Himalayas, which means 'Abode of Snow'. As you move south, you come across the cities of Amritsar, Delhi, Agra, Varanasi (Banaras) and Calcutta. Two large rivers flow across the north Indian plains into the Bay of Bengal – the Jumna (Yamuna) and the Ganges (Ganga), the most holy river for Hindus. Further south are other rivers, such as the Narmada, the Godavari and the Krishna, and other large cities – Bombay on the west coast, and Madras, Mysore and Madurai towards the southern tip of India. Other mountain ranges add to the variety of the landscape. The summer temperature in all parts of India is very high, about 40 degrees centigrade; but it can be cool and pleasant in the mountainous areas. In the north, around Delhi, nights can be very cold in December and January.

In the past, India was ruled first by the Mughals who invaded and occupied Delhi in 1526 CE (Common Era) and then by the British from 1857 CE. However, Indians gained Independence in 1947 and, in 1950, India became a Republic within the British Commonwealth, with an elected Parliament and a President as the Head of State. Today, India has a central government in New Delhi and regional governments in about 18 different states.

The population is nearly 800 million, the majority of which – perhaps 700 million – is Hindu. In spite of this significant Hindu majority, India's democracy is secular, which means that all religions are practised freely and respected equally, with none placed in a position of privilege.

The surface area of India is 1.2 million square miles (3¼ million square kilometres). The national railway network has about 30 000 miles of track, and Indian-made steam and diesel-electric locomotives operate the system, connecting cities which may be 1000 miles apart. Although there are five other countries larger in area, India is called a sub-continent because of its vastness and variety.

Different Images of India

Everyone has a different image of India – they may think of Mahatma Gandhi, of the British Raj or of the rich Maharajas. Some see India as the land of the Taj Mahal and the cricket record-holder Sunil

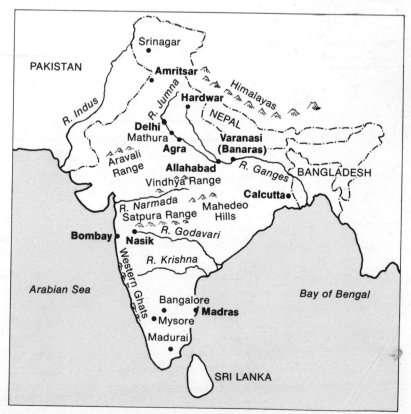

Gavaskar. Others see India as a 'Third World' country sinking in poverty. Some see Indians as hard-working people engaged in trade, agriculture and modern technology. All these images are true and there are many more. India is a land of diversity and contrast, but is united by the two official languages, Hindi and English, by the nationwide railway system and, above all, by its principal religion – Hinduism.

HINDUS OUTSIDE INDIA

Many Hindus have settled in Britain, Canada, the United States and other parts of the world. Those settled in Britain call themselves British Hindus. Although they wear European clothes, speak English as well as their mother tongue and eat English and Indian food, their cultural roots are in India. This is illustrated in the passage below.

A Flight to Bombay

After many years in Britain, I decided to visit India to renew my family and cultural ties. I took a direct flight to Bombay. During the flight I noticed some elderly Hindus eating only vegetarian food and refusing wine or spirits with their meals. The younger Hindus, born outside India, were enjoying their 'Chicken and Chips' and Coca-Cola.

After a nine-hour flight we landed at Bombay at 1 a.m. The monsoons were in full force and, in spite of heavy rain, it was very hot and sultry. I was met by my nephew and his son and we drove to his small flat in the suburbs. When we reached it, at about four o'clock, I took off my shoes and socks, washed my feet and freshened up.

Standing before the small household shrine which was in one corner of the kitchen, I bowed in front of the images of our family deities and offered prayers in thanksgiving for my safe arrival. We all had tea after this simple worship.

---

1   If possible make a large blank map of India to go on the classroom wall. If this is not possible, get a map from a travel agent or shop. Mark on it Delhi, Bombay and Calcutta. Shade the states of Punjab and Gujarat, the states that most Hindus in Britain, East Africa and other parts of the world have come from. Add other places as you find them mentioned in the book.

2   Make a time-line to fit on the wall or in your exercise book. When you work out the scale, remember that it will have to cover about 4000 years, from 2000 BCE to the present day. Put the dates which are included in this introduction onto your time-line and add others as you come across them in your reading.

3   Start to collect photographs of Indian places and people from travel brochures, the *TV Times*, the *Radio Times*, colour supplements, and other magazines. Add some to your map or make a scrap book. Make a separate collection, with newspaper cuttings, about Hindus in Britain.

Part I

The Living Faith

Chapter 1

Worship

There is no standard form of worship in Hinduism; Hindus worship in many different ways, depending on which region of India they come from; on the local climate; whether they live in a city, a town or a village; the social status of their family; whether the act of worship takes place in a temple or at a household shrine. Many deities, representing different aspects of the One God, are offered worship. Underneath this variety, however, lies one common factor: all Hindus begin the day with some kind of religious ritual.

MORNING WORSHIP

The case studies which follow illustrate different forms of worship at the beginning of the day and show how Hinduism is lived in day-to-day life.

Morning in an Indian Town

The town of Shivpur is about 100 miles east of Bombay. Naru was born in Shivpur. He is a Hindu and works as a clerk in the town's law court. He is married and has one son. Raj, Naru's brother, who runs a grocery shop, lives in the same house with his wife and a young daughter. The house is modest, but they have electricity and tap water. The family bathroom is a small room with a stone floor at the back of the house. The whole family gets up early, at about 5.30 a.m. After bathing, they change into cotton clothes, and drink the tea which is normally made by the women of the household. Naru and Raj then go to visit a temple dedicated to Shiva, an important Hindu god, while the women sit in front of the household shrine and offer prayers to various gods and goddesses which are represented by small brass images. The children stand with them at the shrine and join their palms in front of them to say a short prayer.

Sadu works as a mechanic at the bus station. He is unmarried and lives with his parents not far from Naru's house. Sadu and his parents also get up early and bathe. The small shrine in their house has a framed picture of a holy man. Sadu's father performs a simple worship; he cleans the picture, places some flowers in front of it, and lights an incense-stick. All three say their prayers. Sadu then goes out to buy vegetables, while his father goes to the milk-centre where there may be about 50 people queuing up to buy milk.

The town wakes up as Hindus from all walks of life prepare for another day. Bathing is an act of both physical and spiritual cleanliness, and is important to all Hindus. Not everyone in Shivpur goes to the temple each morning, however. Most Hindu rituals are done at home, and visiting the temple is not necessary for a Hindu. A temple may be visited just once a week or only at certain festivals.

Morning in an Indian Village

Over 80 per cent of India's population lives in small villages. These are infinitely varied in pattern, yet there are many features common to all. Devgaon is a small village about 20 miles from Shivpur. The total population is about 1000. Essential services are provided by a barber, a washerman and a grocer. The only teacher of the village primary school also acts as the postmaster. The houses belonging to the rich farmers are newly built, but most villagers live in small houses and the majority are farmers whose fields surround the village. The priest lives at one end of the village and at the other end lives the leather-worker who makes open sandals for the villagers. Devgaon has a temple dedicated to the village deity, and a small stream runs nearby. There is a large well near the temple from which people draw water to carry to their houses.

The villagers, like the people of Shivpur, rise early. Some go to the stream for bathing, others bring water from the well and bathe out in the open, at the side of their houses. Some farmers visit the temple before they set off to work in the fields. The priest bathes in the stream and offers worship to the sun.

Morning in an Indian City

Indian cities are noisy and densely populated. Most people live in small flats and appear to be constantly on the move, going to or returning from work in crowded buses and suburban trains. Private cars and taxis make their own contribution to the noise and movement.

Ramdas lives in Bombay with his wife, Laxmi, and their two young daughters, and runs a taxi, which he owns. They have a two-room flat and in the inner room, where the kitchen is, they have a small household shrine containing a picture of Sai Baba, a holy man. Ramdas gets up early, bathes and offers worship at the shrine using flowers and a joss-stick. After a quick cup of tea, he is at work by 8 a.m. Laxmi and the children offer *namaskar* (see page 4) to the holy man before drinking tea.

Hindus in large cities, like Hindus elsewhere, all begin their day with a religious ritual, rising early, bathing and worshipping at home, at a nearby temple or at a small shrine on the way to work.

Morning for a British Hindu Family

Mr Patel runs a newsagent's shop in Leicester and gets up very early every day to sort out the papers. Before starting work, he has a bath and offers worship to a framed picture of a holy man and to images of deities at the household shrine. After placing some flowers in front of the picture and the images and lighting a joss-stick, he reads a short prayer from a booklet supplied by the local temple. His wife and children also bathe and offer prayers to start their day.

THE MANY NAMES OF ONE GOD

The 'One God' of Hinduism, *Brahman*, is considered to be a Supreme Spirit without any physical form. Hindus are free to imagine the Supreme Spirit in any way that is meaningful to them. The statues or stone images of the One God can thus appear in different forms with various names.

The first aspect of the One God is called Brahma, who created and continues to re-create the world. The second aspect is called Vishnu, who looks after the world. The third aspect is known as Shiva, who destroys a part of the world so that Brahma can continue his work. Brahma, Vishnu and Shiva are the most important names of the One God. The image made to represent all three at the same time is called the *Trimurti*.

The eighteen-foot high Trimurti *image in the Elephanta caves near Bombay; these were excavated 6–8 centuries* CE.

Brahma's wife is Saraswati, the Goddess of Learning and the Arts. Vishnu's wife is Laxmi, the Goddess of Good Fortune. Shiva's wife is Parvati, the female energy in creation. These six gods and goddesses appear in various temples under many different names.

Ganesha, the elephant-headed god, and Hanuman, who looks like a very powerful monkey, are considered as minor but important gods. Other minor gods and goddesses are the village deities, who are very important to the villagers. (Chapter 8 looks at the village deities in detail.)

Personal Experiences

Two years ago I visited the Indian town where I went to high school. The town had changed in many ways; my school was now in a new building and the old bus station had been enlarged. The four temples were as busy as they had been in my school days, and the town's narrow roads were just as dusty. As soon as I arrived at my brother's house, an old school friend came to see me. His name was Madhu. After a long chat and a cup of tea, Madhu suggested that we go for a swim in the river the next morning and then visit some temples. I welcomed the idea, which pleased him.

Early next morning we had our swim and changed into clean cotton clothes. Another man, who had already bathed, was standing in the water on one of the long stone steps at the edge of the river and was offering worship to the rising sun. He took some water in his cupped hands and let it trickle into the river as he looked at the sun. Then he joined his palms in front of him and bowed low, very respectfully. This is called *namaskar*. He offered the river-water 12 times, repeating the 12 Indian names of the sun.

On another step near the water's edge, a woman was offering flowers to the River Goddess. As she dropped the flowers into the water, the current carried them gently downstream.

Madhu and I went to visit the Shiva temple. We took off our sandals and left them outside. As we entered the temple, we reached up and rang the bell and walked up to the door to the inner shrine, the holiest part of the temple. We made our *Namaskars* from the doorway, and as we turned round I noticed a holy man sitting cross-legged in the hall of the temple. He faced the Shiva image, his eyes were closed and his hands rested on his knees. He wore a short loin-cloth, but his upper body and arms were bare. He had a necklace of dried berries (*mala*) round his neck, and as he offered his meditation worship he repeated softly the name of Shiva.

Madhu and I then visited the temple dedicated to Vishnu. Again we left our sandals outside and rang the bell as we entered the temple. We had bought some flowers and a coconut from the stall nearby and we handed these offerings to the priest at the door to the inner shrine. I asked the priest not to break the coconut. He put the flowers on the image and placed the coconut in front. After a few minutes he gave the coconut back to me, saying that it was now blessed and that I should take it back to Bombay as a blessed offering (*prasad*).

Around the inner shrine was a covered path and many people were walking along it. This was their way of offering worship to Vishnu. As they did their circumambulations by walking clockwise round the image, they repeated softly the name of Vishnu. Madhu and I also walked three times round the sanctuary (the holiest part of the temple where the image is).

I was filled with spiritual peace that morning, after bathing, visiting the temples and doing simple acts of worship.

?

Talk to some old people about the changes that have happened in the neighbourhood of your school and in their homes over the last 50 years or more. List what has changed and what has not. Think about change in Indian life. If you can, interview a Hindu who has recently been to his or her hometown or village in India, and check whether your own ideas were correct.

WORSHIP AT HOME

The Household Shrine

If we could take a peep inside almost any Hindu home we would see a shrine containing small metal images of gods and goddesses. In some shrines there are framed pictures of deities and a small copper vessel containing water from the holy river Ganges (Ganga). In Indian villages, a household shrine in a small alcove or in an opening in the wall may contain an embossed piece of copper showing a picture of a local deity. In a small flat in a city, a shrine may be arranged on one side of a shelving unit fixed to the wall.

Image worship is an important aspect of Hindu belief and Hindus use images as symbols of the One God. Most Hindu rituals take place in the home, and though there are different forms of worship, the most common form is called *puja*, in which various offerings are made to an image.

Articles needed for puja

All the articles needed for the daily *puja* are normally put out on a tray near the household shrine. There would be: red *kum-kum* powder and yellow turmeric powder, rice-grains, flowers, fruit, an incense-stick, sandalwood-paste, water, milk and a *ghee*-lamp. In a Hindu holy book, the Bhagavad-Gita, the god Krishna says:

> Whoever offers me, with devotion and a pure heart, a leaf, a flower, a fruit or a little water – I accept this offering.

Cooked food is also offered to the family deities before the midday meal.

A household shrine in Coventry, showing pictures of the goddess Durga and other deities, small images and a puja tray.

A special *puja*, or a 16-stage *puja*, is performed on the annual festival day of any deity. For such a *puja*, additional articles are needed. These include garlands of special flowers, fresh coconut, sacred thread (a loop of five strands of strong cotton thread used in the initiation ceremony, described in Chapter 3), a mixture of milk, yoghurt, *ghee* (clarified butter), honey and sugar, and specially prepared food to be given and received as a blessed offering (*prasad*). A cup and spoon and a small dish, all made of copper, are also needed for this special *puja*.

The 16-stage puja *performed in the home at certain festivals, such as Ganesh-Chaturthi or Durga Puja*

Red *kum-kum*, rice-grains and flowers are always offered to Ganesha, the elephant-headed god, with a prayer that the main *puja* may be performed without difficulty. Similar offerings are made to a water vessel representing the holy rivers; to a conch shell, which is a sacred object; and to a small hand-bell.

The priest says the *mantras*, which are sacred passages of scripture, and the worshipper says a meditation prayer. A small image of the deity in whose honour the *puja* is being held is placed on a bed of rice in a copper dish on a low table in front of the worshipper. The following operations are then performed as the main *puja*:

1   The deity is invited to be present in the image. A blade of grass dipped in *ghee* is held near the image, touching its eyes and heart. The spirit of God is believed to enter the image at this point.

2   The deity is offered a seat. He/She is considered as an honoured guest and is offered welcome as if a human being.

3   Water is offered symbolically for washing the feet. This removes the dust and also cools the body quickly in a hot climate.

4   A water offering is made in reverence.

5   A drink of water is offered. (This is the usual practice in India when a guest comes into the house.)

6   A refreshing bath is prepared. The image is placed in a copper dish on the floor. A spoonful of milk, yoghurt, *ghee*, sugar and honey mixture is poured on the image. Then cold, clean water is spooned onto it as a symbolic bath.

7   The image is dried and placed in the copper dish on the low table. The deity is given fresh clothes which are specially made to fit the image.

8   The sacred thread is placed round the left shoulder of a male deity such as Krishna or Ganesha.

9   The image is anointed with *kum-kum*, turmeric and sandalwood-paste.

10 Flowers and leaves of particular shrubs are arranged round the image.

11 Incense-sticks are lit to create a fragrant atmosphere.

12 A small *ghee*-lamp is lit and waved in front of the image to ward off evil spirits.

13 Food is placed in front of the image. Water for washing hands and mouth and water for drinking is offered to the deity.

14 Fruit and a small cash gift are placed in front of the image. Some betel leaves are offered to aid digestion.

15 Where possible, the worshipper walks round the image as a token of reverence. If this is not possible, the worshipper turns through 360 degrees clockwise with palms joined together and makes salutations in all directions.

16 *Arati* (the conclusion of *puja*) is performed by waving the light in front of the image while verses of praise are sung. These verses praise both male and female deities, since different images and names represent the various aspects of the One God. The priest says the final prayer and, after the worshipper has begged forgiveness of the deity for any omissions in the procedure of the *puja*, the image of the main deity is installed in a specially prepared shrine for the duration of the festival.

Set up a Hindu shrine in your classroom and simulate a *puja*. You are not actually taking part in an act of worship but you are trying to understand what Hindus do and what *puja* means to them. Remember to take off your shoes and sit on the floor. If some of you feel that you cannot join in the simulation, sit behind the others and watch what is happening.

Mandalas

If you lived in an Indian town and went for a walk early in the morning, you would see some of the women sprinkling water outside their front doors and cleaning the threshold. There, and on the ground in front of the house, they would draw various 'good-luck' patterns, called *rangolis*, using coloured powders. More complicated designs, called *mandalas*, are drawn for some of the festivals and *pujas*. They are designed to enable the eye to travel to the centre point, leading the mind from outward diversity towards inner unity. An example of a *mandala* is shown at the top of page 8.

This example of a mandala *shows how, during meditation, thoughts are drawn towards the central point – the source of all existence.*

Aum (Om)

This sacred syllable is made up of three sounds: a, u, m, representing the first three Vedas, the ancient Hindu holy books; the three worlds (Earth, Atmosphere and Heaven); and the three main deities in the Hindu *Trimurti* (Brahma, Vishnu and Shiva). It is believed to contain all the secrets of the universe and is uttered at the start of important passages of scripture in worship, prayer, blessing and meditation. The Sanskrit representation of *Aum* is shown on the left.

Swastika

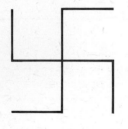

This is a good-luck symbol which means literally 'it is well'. It is believed to have derived from an ancient fire ritual in which the firesticks were always set down in the form of a cross. This equal-armed cross was modified by bending the arms to obtain the symbol shown here on the left. This clockwise swastika is usually drawn in red and is used on wedding invitations, in decorative floor drawings, in textile designs and in various rituals, to bring good luck and to ward off evil spirits.

WORSHIP IN A TEMPLE

Temples

Temples in Indian villages are usually as small as a medium-sized garden shed (see cover, bottom left). They are built of stone or kiln-baked bricks, and have a door, a couple of windows and a spire. The large temples are much more elaborate and, when you study the ground-plans on page 9, you will see that north Indian temples are built to a different design from south Indian ones. The spire (*shikhara*) of a north Indian temple is built directly above the image (*murti*) of the deity, which is in the holiest part of the temple. The tallest part of a south Indian temple, however, is above the main gateway, and its shape is different from the *shikhara* of a north Indian temple. Hindu temples in Britain, as we shall see later, are somewhat different.

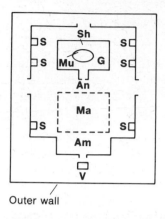

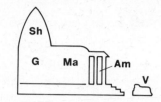

KEY

Mu *Murti* (image of main deity)
Sh *Shikhara* (directly above the *murti*)
G *Garbha Griha* (sanctuary or inner shrine)
An *Antarala* (space between the inner shrine and the main hall)
Ma *Mandap* (pillared hall)
Am *Ardha Mandap* (porch)
S Statues of associated deities
V *Vahana* (vehicle of the deity, for example, Nandi for Shiva, Garuda for Vishnu)

Plan and elevation of north Indian temple.

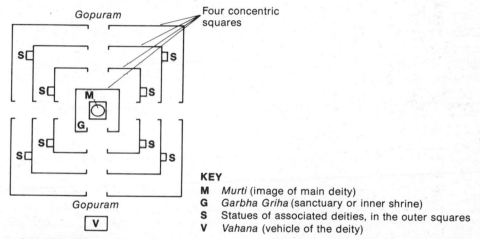

KEY

M *Murti* (image of main deity)
G *Garbha Griha* (sanctuary or inner shrine)
S Statues of associated deities, in the outer squares
V *Vahana* (vehicle of the deity)

Plan of south Indian temple.

Gopuram of a south Indian temple.

Priests

Worship in a temple is conducted by a priest and his helpers, because only they can enter the holiest part of the temple. At festival times, as we have seen with the 16-stage *puja*, some families invite a priest to their homes to conduct the worship.

In British temples the resident priest leads devotions each day, often early in the morning, at midday, late in the afternoon and in the evening, and those who wish may join him at prayer. In the morning he rings the temple bells, prepares the deities, and offers fresh flowers, incense and food which is then received back as *prasad*. Similar worship is offered during the day, along with the prescribed prayers for each service, and in the evening sacred songs are sung by the worshippers, who share in *arati* and *prasad*.

Puja and *Arati* in a Temple – A Personal Experience

Puja

During my recent visit to the Indian town where I went to school, I attended morning worship in a temple. I got up early, bathed, and, wearing clean clothes, I walked to the temple while it was still dark. I sensed the town around me coming to life gradually. Leaving my sandals outside, I went and sat in the temple hall.

The priest and his helper arrived, rang the bell at the entrance and opened the doors to the inner shrine. They removed from the image the flowers and clothes of the previous day, and cleaned the shrine. The priest washed and dried the image and sounded a conch shell to mark the start of the day. The image was anointed with sandalwood-paste, red *kum-kum* and yellow turmeric. Then it was dressed in new clothes and fresh flower garlands. The helper lit incense-sticks and a *ghee*-lamp, and the priest waved these in front of the image. By this time a few more people had arrived to witness the *puja*. The priest then performed the *arati*.

Arati

A special tray had been prepared for *arati*. It had on it a *ghee*-lamp, with five wicks in five separate holders, and some rice-grains. The priest lit the lamp and also some tablets of camphor (a type of oil), which he placed on the rice-grains. He performed *arati* by waving the tray of lights in front of the image, while everyone present joined in the singing of hymns of praise. The priest brought the tray into the hall of the temple and we were able to hold our hands at a safe distance round the flames for a few seconds and then touch our faces to feel the warmth of the sacred light. After everyone had received the sacred light in this way, we were given fresh, sliced coconut and sugar crystals as *prasad*. As a final ritual, the priest prostrated in front of the image in reverence and asked to be forgiven for any omissions in the *puja*.

A worshipper at a London temple offers the arati *tray at the end of a* puja.

Bhajan and *Kirtan* – More Personal Experiences

Bhajan

As the priest left the temple and his helper busied himself sweeping the hall and the front courtyard, a group of about 20 men and women arrived in the temple hall, some carrying tabla drums, small brass cymbals and a harmonium. They sat in two rows facing the deity and began to sing devotional hymns to the accompaniment of the music. I also joined in this *bhajan* and knew the words of one hymn:

> *Hare Rama, Hare Rama, Rama Rama, Hare Hare,*
> *Hare Krishna, Hare Krishna, Krishna Krishna, Hare Hare.*

After the *bhajan* I spoke to the leader of the group, who told me that they perform their *bhajan* sometimes in the temple and sometimes in a private house in the evenings.

Kirtan

The same evening I went back to the temple to attend a religious discourse (*kirtan*) given by a visiting priest who had received special training in that subject. The temple hall was full. Men sat on one side of the priest, women and children on the other. The priest stood facing the image and began his *kirtan* with a prayer. During the first half of the talk, which lasted for about half an hour, he spoke about the importance of doing one's religious duties. In the second half, he told a story to illustrate the moral lesson of duty. The *kirtan* ended with *arati* and *prasad*.

1   If you can visit a Hindu temple, compare what you observe with the author's own experience in India. List similarities and differences. Ask some of the Hindus you meet to tell you whether the differences have any significance or whether they are just another way of doing things.

2   *Prasad* may be an apple, or a piece of apple, a sweet, or sugar crystals and raisins. Why do you think worshippers are given such things?

The Importance of a Temple

In India, as we have seen, a Hindu may visit a temple once a day, once a week, once a month or only at festival times. Most of the important rituals of the Hindu faith are performed in the home, and a visit to a temple is not necessary. A Hindu child learns about purity, *puja*, gods and goddesses, and the various festivals associated with them, by observation and by taking part in rituals at home. When a temple is visited, it is done mainly for the purpose of viewing (*darshan*) the image and offering worship and prayers.

The Temple in Britain

The photographs on page 12 (and on the cover, top left, singing bhajans) show something of the life of a Hindu temple in Britain. Many Hindu temples in Britain are established in private houses, where a couple of rooms are set aside for religious purposes; other temples are found in old church buildings, while others were built specifically as Hindu temples.

Few British Hindu families perform elaborate *puja* at the shrine at home, so the worship ritual at the temple is very important for instructing children in the religious tradition. When a festival is celebrated at the temple, many scattered families come together for the ceremony and people are able to meet their friends, exchange news and renew friendships.

Some Hindu temples run language classes where children are able to learn their parents' language, Gujarati or Hindi, for example; music and dance classes are also held, and facilities are provided for table tennis and other games. Hindu weddings are performed at some temples.

Arati *ceremony*.

Language class.

Laxmi puja.

Concert of Indian classical music.

A temple in Britain is a community centre as well as a place of worship; it is a valued meeting-place, and plays a larger part in the social life of Hindus of all ages than is the case in India.

1   If you were a Hindu living in Britain, why might you travel 50 miles every Sunday to go to the temple, when back in India you might never go to the temple at all? List as many reasons as you can.

2   What kinds of facilities would you want your local temple to provide if you were a Hindu of your own age living in a city where there is a temple which you could visit every day? What kinds of facilities might your parents want the temple to provide for you? What might your grandparents want it to provide for them?

Chapter 2

Pilgrimage and Holy Places

For most people in India, pilgrimages are part of their normal way of life. For example, during certain festivals dedicated to goddess Parvati, the wife of Shiva, people may go on a short pilgrimage to visit the local temple of the deity, or they may visit a shrine of the goddess situated on a hill-top not far from their village. A whole village may be involved, when people of all ages make their way towards the shrine. The physical effort of climbing the hill adds to the spirituality of the experience. Viewing the image of the deity and making offerings of flowers, a coconut and cash at the shrine are the main purposes of such a local pilgrimage. Visiting the shrine on a particular day during the festival has an important religious meaning.

People also go on longer pilgrimages to well-known cities and temples, often spending many hours in a crowded railway train and then completing the journey on foot. A person from a small town near Bombay wishing to go on a pilgrimage to the holy city of Banaras has to travel nearly 1000 miles. Similarly, someone from Delhi wanting to visit a Shiva shrine at the southernmost tip of India will travel an even greater distance.

Certain attitudes and observances are considered important by Hindus. These are:
- showing reverence to religious things and persons;
- self-denial through fasting;
- physical and mental purity;
- charity;
- pilgrimage.

Although pilgrimage is optional for Hindus, it is very popular in India, and certain travel companies and tour-operators specialise in arranging group travel to distant sacred sites and holy places.

REASONS FOR GOING ON A PILGRIMAGE

Apart from the general motive of gaining religious merit, there are certain specific reasons for going on a pilgrimage.

To Bathe

Bathing at a place where holy rivers meet is a religious act for Hindus. A well-known site of pilgrimage for this ritual bathing is Allahabad, a city in north India, where three holy rivers meet. Two of these rivers, the Jumna and the Ganges, have already been mentioned. The third is the Saraswati, which is an underground river. Allahabad is too far away for many Hindus living in central and southern India, so they perform their ritual bathing on full-moon days in October and February in the various regional rivers. Some north Indians bathe on those days in the upper Ganges at Hardwar, north-east of Delhi.

Bathing fairs

Large bathing fairs (*kumbha-melas*) take place every 12 years at Hardwar on the upper Ganges, and at Nasik on the river Godavari, about 120 miles north of Bombay. Bathing at these two places on this special occasion is a matter of deep faith for many Hindus. They undertake the visits in spite of the crush of the large crowds – often as many as 100 000 people – and the somewhat unhygienic condition of the river, for they sincerely believe that a ritual bath during the fairs will wash their sins away and gain them special spiritual merit.

Early morning bathing in the river Godavari, Nasik. A small shrine to Hanuman is in the left foreground.

To Circumambulate

Walking round the main shrine at a place of pilgrimage is an important religious act for many Hindus. The pilgrims always walk in a clockwise direction, so that the shrine is always on their right-hand side. Hindus consider the right-hand side of the body to be ritually purer, and for this reason the right hand is always used for making religious offerings, for eating and for giving and receiving money. At various points along the route to the shrine, pilgrims listen to the guide as he tells them stories from the mythology of the deity. The visitors' names are entered in large ledgers, forming hand-written records which are kept at the temples. Such an entry adds to the prestige of the visitors and their families.

To Make Special Offerings to the Spirits of the Deceased (*Shraddha*)

Many Hindus visit a place of pilgrimage to perform a ritual in which a ball of cooked rice called a *pinda* is offered to the spirit of a deceased relation, usually the father. This is a religious duty for a Hindu and the ritual is called *shraddha* (see Chapter 3).

To Deposit the Ashes of the Deceased in a Sacred River

Hindus believe that the souls of their deceased relations will find peace if their ashes are deposited in a sacred river, particularly the holy Ganges. Many Hindus make a special pilgrimage to Varanasi (Banaras) for this purpose.

To Make Amends

If a person breaks the law of the land, the courts deal with the offence and punish the offender either with a fine or with a term of imprisonment. But if a Hindu breaks a sacred law by acting against a religious rule, that person is required to atone for the sin. Such offences might include the killing of a cow or damaging the image of a deity in a temple. Offenders may have to suffer some physical hardship, give money to charity or perform a special *puja* to the family deities to ask for forgiveness and to ease the troubled mind. The guilt feeling arising from acting against religious rules sometimes leads to physical illness. Atonement of sin is a powerful reason for pilgrimage to certain shrines. One interesting act in the atonement ritual is the 'shadow-gift': repentant sinners look at their reflections in a cup of melted butter and then present the cup as a gift to a priest.

For Faith-Healing

Some believers go on a long journey to a distant shrine in the hope of finding a cure for diseases such as leprosy, which withers and disfigures hands, feet, nose and ears.

Some sects within Hinduism do not allow ritual bathing, the wearing of holy beads and the offering of gifts to holy men at the centres of pilgrimage. In spite of such prohibitions, pious Hindus go on pilgrimages by the thousand.

> **?**
>
> Imagine you are a group of Hindus travelling by train to a pilgrimage centre. Discuss your reasons for going.
> Now imagine you have been. Tell one another how the experience has affected you. (You could divide the class into groups of six and perform your role-play in front of the rest of the class, at a parents' evening or at a school act of worship).

SITES OF PILGRIMAGE

The most popular sites of pilgrimage are the seven holy rivers; five of these, the rivers Indus, Jumna, Ganges (Ganga), Narmada and Godavari, are shown on the map on page vii. The underground river, the Saraswati, is near Allahabad, while the seventh holy river, Kaveri, is north of Madurai in southern India. The river Krishna, although an important river in southern India, is not included in the traditional list of holy rivers.

The mythological story of the Ganges (see below) explains why Hindus consider the Ganges to be the most holy river.

The Story of Ganga

A devotee of Shiva, called Bhagiratha, begged Shiva to allow the sacred river Ganga, which issues from the toe of Vishnu, to descend to Earth from Heaven. Shiva agreed, and from its divine source the river rushed down earth-wards. Shiva, realising its force, caught it in the coils of his thick, long hair, breaking its fall, and allowed it to trickle from his hair down to the Himalayas. As it flowed on Earth, it flooded the sacrificial ground of a holy man, Jahnu, who was angered by the disturbance and drank all its waters. Bhagiratha pleaded with Jahnu, who relented and allowed the river to emerge from his ear. Bhagiratha led the stream carefully over the earth and into the sea and finally underground to the kingdom of the dead. The sacred and purifying waters of the river touched the ashes of his ancestors, who were revived and led into Paradise.

Shiva catches the river Ganga in his hair and allows it to flow down to Earth.

Some important sites of pilgrimage dedicated to the gods Vishnu and Shiva, and to the 'Great Goddess' are shown on the map on page 17.

PILGRIMAGE IN HINDUISM

Religious rituals in Hinduism are of three kinds: essential ones which occur every day, such as making offerings of water to the rising sun or performing *puja* to the family deities at the household shrine; those which are also essential but which take place only on certain special occasions, such as the celebration of the annual festivals dedicated to various gods and goddesses, or the performance of a special thanksgiving *puja* when some happy event takes place in the family; and those which, though considered highly desirable, are optional; one of these is pilgrimage.

Pilgrimage is a religious act performed to experience the spiritual atmosphere of the place visited, or to gain some benefit or blessing. The Hindu word for a pilgrimage is *yatra*, which, before 300 BCE (before Common Era), simply meant travel. As most long journeys undertaken by Hindus at that time were visits to sacred places, the word *yatra* gradually began to be associated with a religious journey or pilgrimage. The Brahmanda Purana, a holy book composed in the ninth century CE, suggests the most suitable times of the year for different pilgrimages and for ritual bathing in sacred rivers, and mentions the various religious acts to be performed at the places of pilgrimage. Still today in modern India Hindus go on pilgrimages to holy places and well-known temples and shrines of different gods and goddesses in order to gain religious merit, to obtain benefit or to give thanks for blessings received.

Major pilgrimage sites of Vishnu, Shiva and 'Great Goddess' shrines. (The map also shows the states of India, so that the pilgrimage sites can be located more easily.)

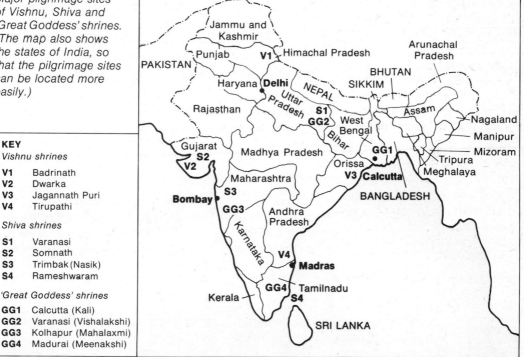

KEY

Vishnu shrines

V1	Badrinath
V2	Dwarka
V3	Jagannath Puri
V4	Tirupathi

Shiva shrines

S1	Varanasi
S2	Somnath
S3	Trimbak (Nasik)
S4	Rameshwaram

'Great Goddess' shrines

GG1	Calcutta (Kali)
GG2	Varanasi (Vishalakshi)
GG3	Kolhapur (Mahalaxmi)
GG4	Madurai (Meenakshi)

1 Write a letter from India to a non-Hindu friend describing a pilgrimage which you have recently made.

2 Not all Hindus regard pilgrimages as important. Construct a discussion between two Hindus with different views on the value of pilgrimage.

3 If possible, persuade one or more Hindus to come and speak to you about what a pilgrimage they have made meant to them.

4 Mark the pilgrimage places mentioned in this section on your map.

Chapter 3

Rites of Passage

THE HINDU FAMILY IN INDIA

Social scientists often use the term 'joint' or 'extended' family to describe the Hindu family. Originally, a typical Hindu family was a household with three or four generations living under one roof, with a common hearth and a common purse. Food was cooked by the women of the family, and shared by all its members; money earned by the men was pooled and allocated according to individual and family needs after consideration by the senior men of the household, sometimes with the informal advice of the elder women. This family structure worked well in the villages, because it ensured a permanent workforce held together by family ties. Property was inherited from father to son and, with the property, went authority, so that important decision-making and power within the family was in the hands of the men, especially the older ones, who had the greatest experience.

Each family member held a place in the family hierarchy of authority and respect, and these positions were emphasised by the roles played by individuals in rituals, by the order in which they sat down for meals (men first, women and children afterwards), and by the terms used to show relationship. In western India, for example, some of these terms are as follows:

Mother: *Ai* or *Mai*   Father: *Baba*
Mother's sister: *Mavashi*   Father's sister: *Attya*
Mother's brother: *Mama*   Father's brother: *Kaka*
Mother's brother's wife: *Mami*   Father's brother's wife: *Kaku*
Mother's or father's father: *Ajoba* Elder brother: *Dada*
Mother's or father's mother: *Aji*   Elder sister: *Tai*

Why do you think European families have so few relationship terms in comparison with Indian ones?

The joint family pattern was not so well suited to industrialised, urbanised, modern India, where young men leave home for higher education or industrial work in towns. Men now set up small family units in flats in the towns where they work and have no room for relatives to stay permanently; and women in the modern Hindu family inherit like their brothers. Nevertheless, the idea of a joint family remains in social, economic and ritual relationships. Young urban couples still see themselves as active members of a larger family unit; they are unlikely to take decisions about changing jobs, buying a flat, arranging a marriage, choosing a career, starting a business and so on without consulting older family members. If a member of the family needs financial support, it is the duty of the other family members to supply it. The expenses of marriages, naming ceremonies, funerals and other life-rituals, as well as of festivals, are shared by the family.

The family, its financial, ritual and social status, its reputation and achievements, are important in determining an individual's place in society. Only males are permanent members of the family unit; women move in or out through marriage, becoming members of their husbands' families (see the diagram below). This does not mean that they break their ties with their original families completely, only that economic and social responsibility for them moves to the family into which they marry. Their position in the new family becomes more influential as the years pass and as their children, especially sons, grow up; the most senior woman of a household can be a figure of authority in family matters, and she will often influence the decisions of the male members.

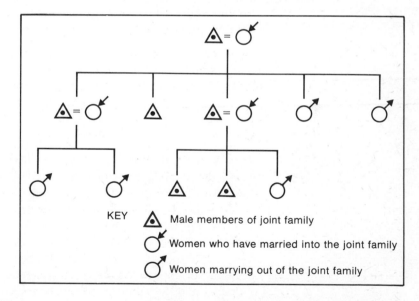

KEY

Male members of joint family

Women who have married into the joint family

Women marrying out of the joint family

1 Imagine you have recently moved to Britain from India with your parents, brothers and sister. What aspects of life in the joint family would you miss? When would you feel the value of the joint family most?

2 Very often most of the joint family will have moved to Britain from India, though members may live in separate houses and even in different towns. What kinds of help could members of the family give (a) a son wanting to start a business; (b) a newly married couple when the husband loses his job; and (c) parents back in India when one of them becomes ill?

LIFE-CYCLE RITUALS

Hindus perform certain rituals to purify the body and to mark the important stages of growth and development throughout a person's life. The Hindu word for such a ritual is *samskara*, which may be translated into English by the word 'sacrament'. Ancient Hindu writers recommend 16 such rituals, but in practice very few people experience all 16. They begin before birth and end with cremation when a person dies. The rest of this chapter looks at the more important of these rites of passage.

Naming a Child

A large majority of Hindu women have their babies at home, and for the first ten days the mother and child come in contact only with the village midwife, a wise practice and precaution against germs and infection. Richer people living in large towns and cities can afford to go to hospitals or maternity homes, where infection is not so common. A child is given a name on the twelfth day after birth, when a naming ritual is performed. The ceremony is usually more elaborate for a boy than for a girl.

In devout Hindu families a priest directs the naming ceremony. The mother and child are dressed in new clothes, and the baby son lies on his mother's lap while she sits on her husband's right. Some rice-grains are evenly spread on a metal plate placed in front of the couple. The father, using a piece of gold wire, writes on the rice-grains the name of their family deity, the son's date of birth and the proposed name of the son. The father whispers this name into his son's right ear. The priest and the elders who are present give their blessings to the child. A cash gift is then given to the priest.

In many families, however, the naming ritual is less elaborate and much more informal. Since women play a major part in the ceremony, it usually takes place in the afternoon when their domestic work is over. The baby is dressed in new clothes and placed in a swinging cot. Twelve lamps are lit and placed below the cot. The name of the child is announced by the eldest woman in the family, and all the women present sing songs in which the new name is inserted at the appropriate place. All the married women are given a handful of cooked pulses, such as chick peas, along with light refreshments. The village goldsmith pierces the earlobes of the child at the naming ritual.

A Child's First Outing

The rite of the first outing is done in the third or fourth month after birth. Its purpose is to make the child aware of its surroundings.

The parents and the child take an early bath on the day of this rite. The father offers simple worship to the family deities at the household shrine. The child, dressed in new clothes, is taken out of the house and made to look at the gentle rays of the morning sun, maybe for a couple of seconds. Care is taken not to damage the eyesight through overexposure. Then, in the case of the village family, the mother and child, accompanied by an older female relative, visit the shrine of the village deity, usually a goddess. The child is dressed in dark clothes, wears a bonnet, and a dab of soot is applied to its cheek and forehead to avert the 'eye of envy' from any childless woman in the locality. (In the past, tropical disease and poor nourishment caused many infant deaths. The 'evil eye' or the 'eye of envy' belief was an attempt to seek an explanation for these deaths when people had very little scientific knowledge.) In the same month, or perhaps a couple of weeks later, on a moonlit night, the child is shown the moon.

First Solid Food

This ceremony is done more elaborately in well-to-do families. On the day of the ceremony, during the morning worship, a special prayer is offered to the family deities, to bring good health and long life to the child. The father feeds the child a small portion of boiled rice mixed with some yoghurt, *ghee* and honey, using a spoon. The feeding is then completed by the mother. In poor families in the villages just boiled rice with some milk is given to the child as its first taste of solid food. The timing of this ritual depends on the health of the child, but usually it takes place seven or eight months after birth. In India, special baby-food in expensive tins is seen only in rich, Westernised families.

The First Haircut

For boys the first haircut is done by the village barber in the fourth, sixth or eighth month after birth. The head is never shorn completely, and a small tuft of hair is left at the front. In some areas of south India this ceremony of the first haircut is also done for girls.

The birth and naming of a child are accompanied by many ceremonies. What value do these ceremonies have for Hindus?

The Rite of the Sacred Thread (*Upanayana*)

Boys from the upper three sections or classes of Hindu society undergo the rite of the sacred thread. This ceremony marks the beginning of a boy's formal education; he begins to learn the Sanskrit prayers which he needs to know in order to represent his family in worship and he starts his training in the responsibilities and duties of an adult member of his family. Unless this ceremony has been performed, he cannot marry. It is the transmission ritual between childhood and adulthood and its ceremonies mark a boy's passing from the care and authority of his mother to the influence and direction of the senior male members of the household. Because of changing social conditions and greater educational opportunities for boys and girls from all sections of society, many Hindus now feel that both boys and girls should experience this sacrament.

Who can perform this ceremony?

The grandfather, father, uncle or any elder male relative of the boy can perform this rite, though in practice it is usually the father.

The ceremony

After a bath on the day of the ceremony, the parents offer worship to the family deities. The best day for the ceremony is chosen by the family astrologer, usually the family priest. The boy's head is shaved, except for a tuft of hair on the crown; he takes a bath, covers his body with a *dhoti* (a piece of cotton cloth about five metres long and a metre wide, used to cover the lower part of the body), and wears a red mark on his forehead. The boy and his mother eat some specially prepared food from the same plate, after which his mother takes no further part in the ceremony. The boy then stands facing west, opposite his father who faces east. A piece of cloth is held between father and son, and songs of blessing are sung.

The worship of sacred fire

A fire is lit in a metal container. Prayers and clarified butter are offered to Agni, the God of Fire, so that the boy may win the right to study the scriptures. He is given new clothes, and a piece of deer-skin on a loop of soft cotton is placed round his neck.

The sacred thread

A loop of strong cotton thread with three or five strands is made sacred by the sprinkling of water, while the Gayatri hymn, taken from a holy book, the Rig-Veda, is chanted ten times. The loop is placed round the boy's head, resting on his left shoulder and hanging below his right hand. His father says, 'May this sacred thread destroy my ignorance, grant me long life, and increase my understanding.' The boy repeats the words as he puts on the sacred thread. The father offers prayers to the Sun God and touches the boy's chest to signify that the boy is now entering the student stage of life (see Chapter 5) and is capable of studying the Vedas (Hindu scriptures).

The priest prepares to place the sacred thread round the neck of the boy undergoing the ceremony.

The Gayatri hymn

The boy kneels on his right knee in front of his father and asks to be taught the sacred Gayatri hymn. He then sits on the floor cross-legged, puts his palms together and places them on his right knee, keeping the right palm above the left. The father covers the boy's hands with a piece of cloth, and recites the hymn slowly so that the boy can repeat it:

> *Om bhur bhuvah swahah. Om tat savitur varenyam bhargo devasya dhimahi. Dhiyo yo nah prachodayat.*

> We concentrate our minds upon the most radiant light of the Sun God, who sustains the Earth, the Interspace and the Heavens. May the Sun God activate our thoughts.

> From the Gayatri hymn, Rig-Veda III.62.10; transliterated and translated by the author.

Advice to the boy

A string of grass is wound round the boy's waist three times and then tied in front. Now he is bound to obey his father, his teacher and the family priest, and to concentrate on his studies. He is given a staff to enable him to follow the right path in his studies. His father then advises:

> Keep your senses under control and keep your body clean. Offer daily prayers to the Sun God and to Agni, the God of Fire. Do not sleep during the day. Obey your teacher. Honour your parents and your nation. Never neglect your studies. Avoid anger and falsehood. Avoid excessive bathing, overeating, and too much sleep. Do not eat or drink anything that will cause harm either to yourself or to others. Show respect to your elders for their experience of life. Work hard to complete this course of study.

> Adapted from the Ashwalayana Grihya Sutra.

The boy pretends to leave home to study the scriptures, but is persuaded to stay for the feast, before which he receives good wishes and presents from his relatives.

What do you think was the purpose and value of the sacred thread ceremony long ago? Is its significance different today?

Marriage

Most Hindu marriages are arranged either through 'matrimonial advertisements' in newspapers (see the examples on page 24), or through recommendations by friends of the family seeking a suitable match for their son or daughter. Very few young men and women choose their marriage partners by themselves. Even where they are

THE HINDU

CLASSIFIED ADVERTISEMENTS

MATRIMONIAL

BRIDEGROOMS WANTED

CORRESPONDENCE INVITED from wellplaced Andhra Brahmin parents of boys below 30 IFS/IAS/IPS/Doctors/Engineers India/abroad for Andhra Brahmin fair, smart accomplished girl 23/165, studying M.S. in U.S.A. Reply with horoscope Box No. 9177, C/o THE HINDU, Madras–600002.

ALLIANCE INVITED for Andhra Brahmin girl 27/168/2500 M.Tech. Doing doctorate in Electronics. Professionally qualified, well-settled executives from metropolitan cities preferred. Reply Box No. 9179, C/o THE HINDU, Madras–600002.

ALLIANCE INVITED from a Tamil Iyer, girl, 33, B.A. Legal divorcee without encumbrance. Box No. 4289 C/o THE HINDU, Madras–600002.

ORIYA GROOM IAS allied Engineer, MBA, C.A. in Khatriya Rajput Khadayat caste for convent educated girl graduate 25/153 respectable family Delhi. Box No. 9219, C/o THE HINDU, Madras–600002.

SOUTH MUSLIM 28 pleasing, pious, Govt. Lecturer invites alliance. Box No. 4281, C/o THE HINDU, Madras–600002.

ALLIANCE INVITED for Kendriya Vidyalaya employed, Post-Graduate, fair, beautiful, Tamil speaking Hindu girl, 33/160cms/2000p.m. from Central, Public School Teachers/Professors/Lecturers/Civil, defence Gazetted Officers/Public or Private Sectors professionals. Province and caste no bar. Reply Box No. 9208, C/o THE HINDU, Madras–600002.

BRIDES WANTED

SYRIAN CHRISTIAN parents settled in USA invite Matrimonial correspondence for their son. 26/168, Computer Programmer doing Masters from Medical doctors, Dentist, Pharmacist or Engineers from Keralite Christians. Box No. 4377, C/o THE HINDU, Madras–600002.

THE TIMES OF INDIA, BOMBAY

TIMES classifieds

ALLIANCE INVITED FOR A TALL, HANDSOME, Parsee boy from Bombay electronics engineer, rank holder, age 24 years, height 181 cms. drawing five figures salary in Gulf, from unorthodox, well educated, fair and attractive girls. Apply to Box P 026–S, Times of India, Bombay 400 001

FOR SUNNI MUSLIM SOPHISTICATED HAND-some intelligent sons: 1) M.A.L.L.M. 28/165 having moderate practice. 2) Under graduate Technologist 25/172 working in Gulf, parents invite matrimonial alliances from educated, beautiful intelligent, goodnatured domesticated maidens from respectable families. Please Write details in confidence Box A 527–K, Times of India, Bombay 400 001

GERMAN GENTLEMAN (BACHELOR) WELL-educated, government-officer, 36 years old, 171 cm tall, well-to-do, seeks very attractive, sharp-featured & slim lady of higher education & decent background for early marriage. Colour, cast & creed no bars. Please submit recent photo along with details to: Mr Joerg Poisson, Alfred Delp str. 2, 7991 Oberteuringen, West Germany.

INDIAN CHRISTIAN HOLDING AMERICAN citizenship aged 48, having own property wants educated girl any caste. Contact Van 1380 S. Yearling road Columbus, Ohio 43227. Phone 614 2378540 America.

These matrimonial advertisements mention religion, class, caste, language and personal details, e.g. 33/160/2000 means age 33, height 160 cm, monthly income 2000 rupees. Horoscopes help to assess the suitability of the couple. Hindus, Muslims, Indian Christians, Parsees and Europeans all advertise for marriage partners in this way.

attracted to each other, their parents make detailed inquiries about the other family to make sure that both families are of equal social, cultural and financial status. The family astrologer then examines the horoscopes of the boy and the girl, and, if the horoscopes are compatible, the parents give their consent and the marriage can go ahead. A lucky day is chosen for the ceremony on the advice of the family priest, a hall is hired for the occasion, and printed wedding invitations are sent to friends and relations. A number of rituals are performed on the day of the wedding and the whole ceremony lasts for about three hours. Special worship is offered to the bride's family deities on the morning of the wedding day.

Engagement

This takes place about a month before the wedding, and the parents of the bride and the groom take an important part in the ritual. The father of the boy formally asks for the girl's hand in marriage to his son. This formal ritual takes place only when most of the senior members of both families have agreed to go ahead with the marriage. In some families, both sets of parents stand facing each other, all holding hands, and agree to let their respective son and daughter marry each other.

On the day of the wedding, 15 different rituals, showing important points in the Hindu marriage, are performed:

The marriage ceremony

1   **The bridegroom is welcomed**   The bridegroom arrives for the wedding. He is welcomed by the bride's parents at the entrance to the house where the wedding will take place.

2   **A drink of welcome**   After the ceremony at the door, the bridegroom is offered a mixture of milk, *ghee*, yoghurt, honey and sugar as a drink of welcome.

3   **Private worship of Parvati**   While the bridegroom is being welcomed, the bride offers worship to goddess Parvati, the wife of Shiva. She prays for a long and happy married life for herself and her future husband. The bridegroom does not see this private worship.

A bride offers private worship to Parvati before the wedding ceremony.

4   **Songs of blessings**   The bride and the bridegroom stand facing each other. A silk cloth is held between them by the priest and his assistant to form a curtain. On the silk cloth, swastika and *Aum* symbols are drawn in red. Rice-grains tinged with red *kum-kum* powder are distributed among the guests. Specially designed flower garlands are worn by the couple. Songs of blessings are sung and, at the end of each verse, the guests shower the couple with rice-grains.

5   **The daughter is given in marriage**   The daughter is formally given in marriage by her father to the bridegroom. The bride's father asks the groom to

promise to be moderate in the observance of his moral duty (*dharma*), the earning of money (*artha*), and the enjoyment of good things in life (*kama*). The bridegroom repeats his promise three times.

6 **Sprinkling with gold**   A copper vessel is filled with cold water and a gold ring is put in it. The priest dips a flower in the water and lightly sprinkles the couple. This is supposed to bring good fortune in their married life.

7 **Symbolic bond**   A piece of soft cotton thread is rubbed with yellow turmeric and tied, separately, round the wrists of the couple. Now they are bound together for life.

8 **Blessed rice-grains**   The priest utters verses from the scriptures (*mantras*) and blesses a small quantity of rice-grains. The couple shower each other with blessed rice as a symbol of purification.

9 **The marriage necklace (*mangala sootra*)**   The bridegroom and his mother tie round the bride's neck a necklace of black beads and two gold hemispheres strung on gold wire. This tells the world that a woman is married; rings are not used by Hindus as symbols of marriage. A married Hindu woman also wears a red mark on her forehead during her husband's lifetime.

10 **The sacred fire (*homa*)**   Now the couple worship the sacred fire by making offerings of grain and clarified butter.

11 **Holding the wife's hand**   The husband holds his wife's hand and accepts her as his lifelong friend and companion.

12 **Roasted rice offerings**   The couple offer some roasted rice or popcorn to the sacred fire. After this, the bride's brother pretends to twist the right ear of the bridegroom to remind him of his duty and responsibility towards his bride. The bridegroom promises to do his duty faithfully and gives a small cash present to his brother-in-law. This act frees the wife from ties to her father's family; now she has obligations to her new family.

13 **The seven steps**   The couple walk seven steps, taking a vow for each step, with the wife following the husband. The husband says, 'Take the first step, follow me in my vows, may God be your guide.' This *mantra* is repeated, first by the priest, then by the husband. 'Take the second step for power; the third for prosperity; the fourth for happiness; the fifth for children; the sixth for the enjoyment of seasonal pleasures; and the seventh step for a close union and lifelong friendship.' A Hindu marriage is not binding until after the seven-steps ritual.

14 **Viewing the Pole Star**   The couple stand facing the north and look at the Pole Star together. The wife promises to be constant, like the Pole Star, in her new family and not to stand in the way of her husband's good and righteous actions.

15 **The blessing**   The couple are blessed by the priest for a long and prosperous married life. Friends and relations offer good wishes and give presents at the reception. The assembled guests then enjoy a grand dinner.

1 Most marriages in India are 'arranged', though 'love marriages' are not unknown. (This applies to Christians as well as to Hindus, Sikhs and Muslims). What things would a family take into account when looking for a suitable husband or wife for their child? (You may wish to reconsider your answer after reading Chapter 13.)

2   Why might Hindus (and others) still prefer arranged marriages to love marriages in today's world? Discuss this with a partner, one pretending to be a Hindu who favours arranged marriages, the other a Hindu who prefers a love marriage. (NB Hindus insist that the couple should consent voluntarily to the choice of partner.)

3   Simulate a Hindu wedding.

A Hindu Cremation

The following letter, which was received by a Hindu student in London, is reproduced with the writer's permission.

Satara, 3rd March

My dear Gopal,

Since you went to London to study for an M.Sc. degree, Baba, our father, had been in good health; therefore I am sure you must have had a shock when I telephoned you last week to say that he was dead. His death was caused by a road accident. I would never have thought that such a thing could happen in a small town like Satara, but it did. Baba was travelling in a motor-rickshaw which collided with a State Transport bus. The rickshaw-driver and Baba both died, but nobody else was seriously injured. Of course the bus was badly dented at the front, but the bus-driver escaped unhurt.

The police arrived on the scene and found out that the rickshaw was overtaking a bullock-cart when it crashed head-on into the oncoming bus. I was informed of the accident within ten minutes, when I was in the middle of a lesson. I spoke to the Headmaster who told me to take the rest of the day off, so I left school and went to the scene of the crash.

When the police had confirmed that Baba's death was the result of an unfortunate accident, Dr Joshi signed the death certificate and I brought our father's body home. By this time the news had reached many friends and neighbours, and when I arrived home there were ten or twelve people waiting to offer sympathy and help in the funeral arrangements. Normally you, being the eldest son, would have performed the final rites, but since you were far away in London I did this in your place, although I am not even the youngest brother; our youngest brother, Rama, was in Madras on a tour of inspection of the Railway Depot there.

Our two neighbours on either side were most helpful in this hour of grief. They came with me to the fuel seller to buy the wood fuel and the cow-dung slabs. The fuel seller and his assistant filled the cart with the fuel and promised to take it to the cremation ground. I paid him 100 rupees, and we also collected the bamboo and string to prepare a stretcher for Baba's final journey. In Bombay the dead can be taken to the cremation ground by ambulance, but in Satara such things are not available.

Baba's body was bathed, and dressed in new dhoti and shirt. When the stretcher was prepared, we put the body on it and covered it with a new piece of white cloth, leaving the face uncovered. A garland of red flowers was placed round the neck of the corpse.

Our family priest then asked me to put some live embers in an unglazed earthen pot; they were to be used for lighting the pyre. Four neighbours wound old dhotis round their heads as funeral turbans and lifted the stretcher so that Baba's feet were pointing in the direction of the journey. I carried the earthen pot and walked in front of the corpse. Throughout the twenty-minute walk we all chanted the name of God Rama.

When we arrived at the cremation ground, the cart with the fuel was waiting for us. The logs were arranged to construct the pyre in such a way that the layer above was at right angles to the layer below. When the pyre was ready, Baba's body was placed on it, his head pointing to the north. Three neighbours arranged the cow-dung slabs round the head of the corpse to create maximum heat, which would crack the skull without any human effort. The priest chanted verses from the Vedas and the Bhagavad-Gita, our holy book, to sanctify the fire. I was asked to light the pyre using the embers which I carried. When that was done, the priest drilled a tiny hole in the bottom of the pot, filled it with water and asked me to carry it round the pyre. As I did so, water dripped on to the ground, forming a line. This was done three times to prevent Baba's soul from returning to Earth and haunting the living. Soon the pyre blazed on all sides and we all sat at a distance and watched it.

The funeral pyre described in the letter would have looked similar to the one shown here at Udaipur, Rajasthan.

We waited for nearly an hour before the skull cracked and then, when the priest assured me that Baba's soul would escape skywards, we all returned home. The attendant at the cremation ground was paid 20 rupees to watch the fire to make sure that the entire body would be completely burned to ashes.

Three days later, the priest and I went to the cremation ground and collected some ashes and small pieces of bone in an earthen pot. The rest was thrown in the river. Soon I shall send these ashes to Banaras and the priest there will deposit them in the river Ganges. For ten days we were in mourning; I did not shave during that period and no sweet dish was prepared in the house.

I hope you have got over the shock of our father's death. I am sure it was difficult for you to come to terms with our great loss, especially as you are far away from our relations. I am sure you will control your grief and finish your studies successfully.

When you return to India next year, it will be the first anniversary of Baba's death. Our family priest has suggested that both of us should travel to the holy city of Banaras and perform the shraddha ceremony and give some money to charity. If we do this ceremony at Banaras our father's soul will find peace. Of course we shall give 101 rupees to a deserving schoolboy each year to remember Baba.

Our mother's grief cannot be described in words, and it will take a long time for her to accept the situation and begin to lead a fairly normal life. She sends her blessings and good wishes for your success.

Your affectionate brother,

Krishna

Shraddha

This family ceremony marks the anniversary of death. Balls of cooked rice (called *pinda*) are offered for the welfare of the spirits of the deceased and then distributed among the guests, many of whom will be Brahmins.

The Hindu family prepares the body for cremation and performs the rituals. How does this help them cope with the death of a loved one?

FAMILY CEREMONIES IN BRITAIN

For Hindus in Britain, the most important of these ceremonies are the naming ritual, marriage and cremation. Devout families also observe *shraddha*. Priests officiate at all these rituals which, while following the traditional outline, may vary according to regional and family practice.

How do the different rites of passage help bind together the Hindu family?

Chapter 4

Festivals

Hindu festivals are colourful and happy occasions. The celebrations encourage the continuance of religious traditions and enable Hindu children to learn about the various deities to whom the festivals are dedicated. Some festivals are regional in emphasis, others have an all-India appeal. Some involve fasting and private worship in the home, while others are celebrated as public festive occasions, with the whole community taking part.

FOUR BIRTH-FESTIVALS

The birth of a baby is an occasion of great joy for families everywhere. Hindus celebrate the birth-festivals of four deities with great enthusiasm and sincere faith.

Prince Rama

Prince Rama is an incarnation of Vishnu, and the anniversary of his birth is celebrated at noon on the ninth day (*navami*) of the first month of the Hindu calendar. Where possible, people gather for this event in a Rama temple, with songs of praise and the distribution of a blessed offering (*prasad*). The festival is known as *Rama-Navami*.

Hanuman

On the day of the full moon in the same month, the birth of Hanuman, the monkey-god, is celebrated just before sunrise. Many villages in India have temples dedicated to Hanuman.

Narasimha

At sunset on the fourteenth day of the second month of the Hindu calendar, the birth of the man-lion (Narasimha), another incarnation of Vishnu, is celebrated. God Vishnu, who looks after the world, is believed to have appeared on Earth in many incarnations to save humanity.

Lord Krishna

The birth of Lord Krishna, who is also an incarnation of Vishnu, is celebrated as a festive occasion not only by Hindus in India, but also wherever Hindus have settled outside India. The celebration, known as *Janma-Ashtami*, takes place at midnight on the eighth day (*ashtami*) of the dark fortnight in the month of *Shravan* (the fifth month of the Hindu calendar). The event is remembered either at home at the family shrine or in a Krishna temple as an act of collective worship, when the story of Krishna's birth is read by a priest. The story is recorded in three of the books of Hindu legends, the Puranas (see Chapter 12), but the most popular version occurs in the Bhagavata Purana.

RAKSHA-BANDHAN

This festive occasion is celebrated on the day of the full moon in the month of *Shravan*. Women tie a red silk thread with a bauble strung on it round the right wrist of each of their brothers. This thread is called a *raksha* or a *rakhi*, and the actual binding (*bandhan*) symbolises the renewal of ties of affection. Friends also exchange these silk threads to renew their friendship. In the coastal towns and villages of India, people throw coconuts into the sea as an offering to the Sea God, and a sweet dish containing fresh coconut is prepared for the midday meal.

Rakhis on sale at Loi Bazaar, Vrindaban.

GANESH-CHATURTHI

Hindus of western India celebrate the Ganesha festival in their homes as well as publicly with a neighbourhood festival. The festival begins on the fourth day in the light half of *Bhadrapad*, the sixth month of the Hindu calendar. A clay image of Ganesha is brought home the previous day from the local sculptor. It is very colourful and shows the god with an elephant's head, and four arms. Ganesha is the remover of obstacles; hence he is worshipped at the beginning of every Hindu *puja*, at the start of any undertaking or before a long journey.

Celebrating Ganesha at Home

On the first day of the festival the head of the family performs an elaborate *puja*. The Ganesha image is then installed in an alcove which has been freshly painted and decorated with tinsel, brightly coloured paper and, in some households, electric lights of different colours. At the morning and evening worship the image is not moved, since it is believed to possess the spirit of God. This home-based festival lasts for two, five, seven or ten days depending on the family tradition.

Public Celebration of Ganesha

The public festival brings together all Hindus in the neighbourhood to worship the image of Ganesha. It is one example of group worship in Hinduism.

The image is installed in a temporary pavilion made of bamboo, light timber and tarpaulin. The shrine is built on a raised platform and decorated with tinsel and coloured paper. Morning and evening worship is performed by an important person in the community and after the evening *arati* some specially prepared food is distributed as *prasad*.

This public festival normally lasts for ten days, and each night some form of entertainment is arranged: a short play performed by the young people, or a concert of film songs, for example. Occasionally, if enough money is collected, a well-known musician is invited to play an Indian musical instrument or to sing classical Indian music. There may be an evening of folk-dances or folk-songs and the local schools may hold competitions in public-speaking or essay-writing.

On the tenth day the image is taken in procession to the river, joined along the way by all the other images from various communities in the town. After the final *arati*, the Ganesha image is dipped in water three times and thrown into the river.

NAVARATRI

This 'Nine-Nights' festival begins on the first day of *Ashwin*, the seventh month of the Hindu calendar, and worship is offered to goddess Parvati, the wife of Shiva. Some Hindus celebrate this festival with great devotion. In the household shrine a small brass image of Parvati is installed on a bed of rice in a copper dish and *puja* is performed twice a day. An oil lamp is lit and kept burning day and night for nine days. Each day a single-strand garland of seasonal flowers, such as marigolds, is hung from a peg above the image. Special food is offered to the deity at midday.

During Navaratri, some Hindu families get together each night in a local hall to enjoy 'stick-dances' (folk-dances in which short sticks are knocked together to keep time) and devotional songs in praise of the goddess.

'Stick-dances' being performed at the Shree Krishna temple, Coventry, during Navaratri.

A priest conducting Durga puja before the image of the deity in Gopinath Bazaar, Vrindaban.

DURGA PUJA

Durga, another name of Parvati, represents the war-like aspect of the goddess. This festival is celebrated with great enthusiasm in Bengal in north-east India and by Bengali Hindus everywhere. It is celebrated as a public festival in Bengal in much the same way as the Ganesha festival is celebrated in western India. A large clay image of Durga, with eight arms holding different weapons and riding a tiger, is installed on a raised platform, and the main *puja* is offered on the eighth day of the Navaratri celebrations. At the end of the festival, the image is taken in procession through the town and thrown into a river.

DUSSERAH

This important festival which celebrates events from the two great Hindu epic poems the Ramayana and the Mahabharata (see Chapter 11 for details), occurs on the day after Navaratri. Traditionally, in north India, the exploits of Prince Rama, known as Rama Leela, against Ravana, the King of Lanka, are celebrated with public gatherings and displays of fireworks. Large figures of Ravana and his helpers, made from bamboo and paper, are blown up with the fireworks. This Rama Leela festival shows other events in the Rama story on earlier days, but the final destruction of Ravana takes place on Dusserah day.

In western India, an incident from the Mahabharata, which tells the story of the Pandu princes, is celebrated. People dress up in their best clothes and go to the edge of their village or town to exchange the leaves of the tree mentioned in the story. This is a symbolic renewal of ties of friendship, when class barriers are forgotten. It is a feast day and a sweet dish is always prepared for the midday meal. Dusserah is considered a lucky day.

The Story of the Pandu Princes

The five Pandu princes have lost their share of the kingdom in a gambling match to their cousins, the Kuru princes, and as a result they are forced to leave their palace and live in the forest for 13 years. During the final year of their exile, they have to be certain that they are completely unrecognised by everyone and, to make sure of this, they hide all their weapons in a hollow tree. The princes have richly ornamented weapons, such as can only belong to members of the royal family; these would betray their identity. When a year has passed by, at the time of Dusserah, the Pandu princes collect their weapons and prepare to do battle with their cousins to win back their half of the kingdom.

DIWALI

Diwali is celebrated over five days, normally during the third or fourth week of October. In India, schools and colleges have a long holiday at this time and office workers get two days' leave in the middle of the festival. It is therefore possible to perform various rituals and ceremonies throughout the five-day period. In Britain and North America, Hindus celebrate Diwali on only one evening; the festivities include fireworks for children and a lavish dinner for everyone. Various Hindu clubs and temples arrange this Diwali dinner on the Saturday evening nearest to the actual days of Diwali.

In India, the festival is celebrated in a variety of ways in different parts of the country, but usually the following rituals are performed:

The first evening
A single flame lamp is offered to Yama, the Spirit of Death. The flame points towards the south, the quarter over which Yama rules.

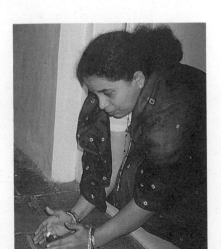

A single-flame lamp is offered to Yama, the Spirit of Death, at the start of Diwali festivities in Bombay.

The second day

People rise early and have a ceremonial bath after their bodies have been rubbed with perfumed oil. After the bathing ritual, friends and neighbours enjoy specially cooked dishes for breakfast. *Puja* is offered to Vishnu to celebrate his victory over the demon Naraka.

The evening of the third day

This is the last day of *Ashwin*, when Laxmi, the Goddess of Wealth and Good Fortune, is worshipped. Silver coins, gold ornaments, banknotes, cheque-books and business account-books, representing Laxmi, are offered *puja*. Fireworks are lit, buildings are 'floodlit' by oil lamps, people wear new clothes and enjoy a feast after the *puja*. The financial year comes to an end and new account-books are started the next day.

The fourth day

Every husband is supposed to give a present, usually a sari, to his wife, and the children also get new clothes. This is a day of new beginnings, since it is considered a lucky day. Worship is offered to Vishnu to celebrate his victory over a tyrant named Bali.

The final day of Diwali

This is called 'sister's day'. Men visit their sister's house, enjoy a feast, and honour their sister with a present.

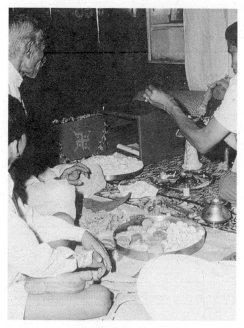

Laxmi puja at a research institute in Vrindaban. A priest draws a red swastika on the cash-box of the organisation, which is presented to the goddess for blessing.

Hindu children often say, 'Diwali is our Christmas,' because of the rich food and exchange of presents and greetings cards. This comparison of Diwali to Christmas is, however, rather misleading; the origins of the festivals are quite different and the ways of celebrating them only superficially similar.

MAHASHIVA-RATRI

Strictly speaking Mahashivaratri is neither a festival nor a feast. It is a fast, when the devotees of the great god Shiva go without food for 24 hours and offer worship to his image. Those who are not able to observe a complete fast are allowed to eat certain foods such as sago, potatoes, peanuts, fruit and milk.

This special fast is kept on the day before the new moon at the end of the Hindu month of *Magha* (February). Worship is offered to Shiva between midnight and sunrise, by repeating his name and placing flowers and grain on the Shiva image. Water is offered in a steady stream from a copper vessel suspended over the image. At the end of this vigil the worshipper returns home from the temple and, after bathing, breaks the fast of *Maha-shiva-ratri*.

The devotees of Shiva, who consider him the most important deity, explain the importance of selfless devotion to Shiva:

> If you offer worship to Shiva, His name will cleanse all your sins; you need not study the Vedas and other holy books; you need not go on a pilgrimage; the practice of Yoga and various religious observances then become unnecessary; you need not fear the wicked and Death itself will not frighten you.

Extract from a hymn praising Shiva, based on the Skanda Purana; translated by the author.

HOLI

This festival is celebrated both privately and publicly on the day of the full moon in *Phalgun* (March), the last month of the Hindu calendar. Holi is a spring festival in which the Indian farmers take full part in a carefree manner after the spring harvest is safely gathered in. In middle-class homes *puja* is offered to a small bonfire before the midday meal, when a portion of the special food is thrown into the fire in thanksgiving.

The neighbourhood bonfire is made by the local men and boys. They visit all the houses to collect wood and other rubbish, which is then taken to a piece of open ground. Some people also give money to help buy coconuts to be roasted and used as *prasad*. The bonfire is lit as soon as darkness falls. When the fire is blazing, people walk round it as a token of reverence, and before going home they streak their foreheads with ash to bring them good luck during the coming year. People throw small coins into the fire and roast coconuts at the edge of the bonfire; they eat the copra (the kernel of a coconut) as *prasad*.

In villages, men play various games the following day and children play with coloured water, squirting it on friends and strangers in fun. Young and old, men and women, all join in the merriment, and when the colourful ammunition is finished, they bathe and change into clean clothes. In some parts of India this playing with coloured water and powders takes place five days after the Holi bonfire.

RATHA-YATRA

Ratha-Yatra (which means 'chariot procession') usually takes place at the end of the annual festivals of the various deities. A wooden image of a deity, normally kept in a storehouse, is dressed in ceremonial garments, garlands and a crown, and taken in procession in a chariot along the same route every year. The consecrated stone image of the deity cannot be used for the procession as it is fixed on a stone plinth in the inner shrine of the temple. The wooden image, however, enables the devotees to offer worship as the chariot passes their houses, and a number of stops are made along the route for this purpose. The devotees wave a lighted lamp in front of the image in the chariot from a spot as near to it as possible, and throw flowers and unshelled groundnuts at the chariot. Passers-by rush forward and pick up the groundnuts as *prasad*.

Famous *ratha-yatras* take place annually at the Jagannath temple at Puri on the east coast of India and also at Udipi in Karnataka State on the west coast. One of the pictures on the cover of this book (top right) shows some of the chariots at Udipi being pulled through the crowds of pilgrims. The chariot procession at Puri takes place in June or July each year. The chariot is 13½ metres high and 10½ metres square, with 16 wheels each 2 metres in diameter. Over 4000 men are needed to pull the chariot. Each year the chariot is broken up and an exact replica is built the following year. Today, heavy lorries are called juggernauts because of their similarity in size to the chariot of Jagannath. (Another picture on the cover of this book [bottom right] shows *ratha-yatra* in Bradford, Yorkshire.)

If a special procession is organised in a particular area to mark an important event, the image of the local deity is also taken in procession in a chariot. As we have seen, at the end of the Durga and Ganesha festivals, clay images of these deities are taken in procession in small chariots, mounted on lorries, to be thrown into the local river. These processions, though not annual events, are similar to the *ratha-yatras*.

SARASWATI PUJA

A festival in honour of Saraswati, the Goddess of Learning and the Arts, is celebrated on the fifth day of the eleventh month of the Hindu calendar. This day normally falls in the first week of February. It may be a family worship in the home or a neighbourhood public festival involving the whole community. The celebration is similar to Durga Puja or the Ganesha festival, and includes the consecration of the image, performance of *puja* and *arati*, followed by a feast and the immersion of the clay image in water. It is a regional festival, very popular in Bengal but seldom observed in other parts of India. It is celebrated in Britain and North America by Hindus from Bengal who have settled there.

A VILLAGE FAIR

In addition to the popular festivals of Diwali and Holi, every large village where the local market is held celebrates an annual fair dedicated to the guardian deity of the village. This deity is usually a goddess, who is looked upon by the villagers as their mother (*mata*).

The shrine of the goddess is cleaned and decorated with leaves strung on strong cotton thread. The image of the deity is dressed in new clothes and a crown, and *puja* is performed by the village headman. A wooden image, similarly dressed, is then taken in

The 'Big Wheel' at an Indian village fair. Chapter 8 describes the religious significance of such fairs and festivals in more detail.

procession through the village at night, with village musicians and drummers leading the way. People offer flowers, coconuts or unshelled groundnuts to the deity as the procession passes their houses.

On the second day of the fair, folk-singers, folk-dancers, jugglers and tight-rope walkers provide entertainment between 10 a.m. and 2 p.m. After a late lunch, all the villagers and visitors from the smaller surrounding villages gather in a field where no crops are growing. They sit on all four sides of the field to watch wrestling contests. Many of the wrestlers bring small clay images of Hanuman, and bow to him before their contests, since Hanuman is the patron of physical strength and fitness.

The competitors are divided into three groups according to age and experience: Boys, Youths, and Veterans, and the winner of every match gets a colourful turban as a prize. The most expensive turbans are awarded to the champions in each group.

These village fairs are held when the harvest is safely gathered in. They are important local festivals, not only honouring the mother goddess of the village, but also giving village entertainers and sportsmen a chance to gain fame and prestige.

?

1   Imagine you live in an Indian village. Choose one of the festivals described in this chapter and write about it in a letter to a friend. Explain why and how it is celebrated.

2   Explain why Hindus in Britain tend to celebrate fewer festivals and observe them in their homes and temples rather than outdoors.

3   Try to visit a Hindu temple to join in one of the festival celebrations. They usually take place in the evening or at weekends, and you would be very welcome. Talk with Hindus about it and then write a letter to a friend describing and explaining it. Try to convey the atmosphere.

Chapter 5

A Way of Life: Varna-Ashrama-Dharma

As we have already seen, the words 'Hindu' and 'Hinduism' were used by foreigners to refer to the people on the other side of the river Indus and to their religion, respectively. Hindus themselves refer to their way of life as 'the ancient, or eternal, religion' (*Sanatana-dharma*). This ancient religion is also called *varna-ashrama-dharma*, a term which refers to the duties of a way of life based on *varna* (social class) and *ashrama* (a particular stage in life). The *varna* duties of a Hindu remain unchanged throughout life, but duties arising from age (*ashrama* duties) change as the person grows older and passes through various stages of life. A Hindu has other duties, too, such as telling the truth, avoiding harm to others, respecting other people's property and not cheating.

The word *dharma* really means more than 'duty'; it includes the discipline and responsibilities of life which are essential for the support and protection of the individual, the family, and society.

VARNA

The word '*varna*' is used to denote social class, though its literal meaning is 'colour'. The Aryan people who invaded India in about 1500 BCE were light-skinned nomadic warriors. As they settled in their new land they had to conquer the original inhabitants who were darker in colour. Aryan society was divided into three classes or *varnas*: Brahmins (priests, professionals), Kshatriyas (rulers, administrators, soldiers) and Vaishyas (peasant-farmers, merchants). Scholars believe that these social classes were not rigid divisions; people were able to move into an upper or lower *varna* according to their skills and abilities. Later on a fourth *varna*, Shudras, was added. These were skilled people such as weavers, potters and basket makers, who served the three upper *varnas*. Each individual's duty was to perform the work of his *varna* to the best of his ability.

As Aryan rule became more dominant in India and more of the original inhabitants were absorbed into Aryan society, the divisions between classes became more rigid. A fifth class eventually evolved at the very bottom of the scale, made up of the people who did the dirtiest jobs in society, such as working with leather, or removing dead cattle and other rubbish. The upper *varnas* treated them inhumanely, even avoiding their touch. These 'untouchables' were the most oppressed section of society. A famous Hindu, Mahatma Gandhi (see Chapter 16), hoping to improve their social position, named them Harijans – the 'Children of God'.

The constitution of India has now abolished the practice of untouchability in any form. Nevertheless, the social status of the Harijans has not improved, in spite of preferential treatment given to them in education and government jobs. They do not like the word *harijan* and prefer to call themselves *dalit* (depressed).

Industrial development in India has created opportunities for new types of jobs which are open to all. This means that people from different *varnas* are found in jobs which are not their traditional occupations. Brahmins now work as taxi-drivers, machine-operators, airline pilots or priests. They also run cafés and restaurants, work in the professions and run businesses. People from other *varnas*, including the *dalits*, are employed in similarly varied occupations. Former class barriers are disappearing in large cities and towns, but the 3000-year-old system is not likely to disappear in 30 or 40 years, even though many changes are taking place.

The classification based on occupation within each social class is dealt with in more detail in Chapter 13.

ASHRAMA: THE FOUR STAGES OF LIFE

A Hindu's life is divided into four distinct stages (*ashramas*). Each *ashrama* brings its own special duties.

The First Stage (*Brahmacharya-Ashrama*)

Brahmacharya, the first or student stage, begins with the initiation rite called *Upanayana* or the rite of the sacred thread. Boys belonging to the three upper *varnas* undergo this ceremony, signifying a second birth, and are called 'twice-born'. Nowadays very few boys actually attend the traditional schools to study the scriptures and train to become priests; most boys and girls attend Western-type primary and secondary schools in towns and cities and study to learn skills for their future employment. A student's duties are to gain knowledge by following a course of study, to show regard to teachers and parents for their experience of life, and to learn the various rules and rituals of the Hindu tradition.

The Second Stage (*Grihastha-Ashrama*)

After acquiring a skill and getting a job, a young Hindu marries and enters the second stage of life, that of a married householder. The Hindu word for this stage is *grihastha-ashrama*. Getting married and having children is considered a sacred duty, in order to continue the family and, with it, social and religious traditions. A householder is expected to celebrate festivals, perform various rituals, give to charity, offer hospitality to guests and care for aged parents. A settled, well-run household is essential for social stability. A Hindu marries only one person at a time; in modern India divorce is possible. A married woman's duties include bringing up children, managing the household expenses, preparing food, keeping the home clean, offering hospitality to guests and organising the celebration of festivals and other religious rites. Many Hindu women have a full-time job as well. A man must provide for his wife and children, educate and arrange marriages for his sons and daughters, earn money honestly and spend it in ways which will not cause harm either to himself or to others.

A retired airline pilot enjoys the company of his grandson.

The Third Stage (*Vanaprastha-Ashrama*)

The third stage of life is known as *vanaprastha-ashrama*, which literally means 'forest-dwelling stage'. In modern Hindu society, this means retirement from daily work after a man has fulfilled all his social, religious and family obligations and secured a pension. He hands over the running of the household to his son and spends his time studying his favourite holy books. He may decide to go on a pilgrimage. He is often called upon to give advice on certain matters because of his experience. In the villages, such men are much respected. Women do not deliberately enter this stage of life, though some may hand over the running of the household to a daughter-in-law.

The Fourth Stage (*Sannyasin*)

The fourth stage is that of a *sannyasin*. A *sannyasin* gives up all ties to worldly life, his family name and most of his belongings, and becomes a wandering holy man. He meditates upon the mysteries of death and rebirth. He has very few belongings and begs for food. When he dies, he is buried, because there is nobody to perform the funeral rites and cremation. This stage is optional and very few men enter it. Women do not become *sannyasinis*; it is not socially acceptable in India for women to wander the country alone, and such an action would prevent a son from fulfilling his *ashrama* duty towards his mother.

1   What advantage can you see in the Hindu tradition of dividing life into four parts (*ashramas*)?

2   Imagine you are seriously thinking of entering the fourth stage of life. Hold a conversation with your wife, son and daughter, and ask them for their views to help you make up your mind.

THE FOUR AIMS OF HUMAN LIFE

For over 2500 years Hindus have had four basic aims in life, which make up a personal value system for each individual. The concept of *dharma*, or religious duty, is one of these aims. The four basic aims are:

- Faithfully carrying out religious and social duties, thus disciplining other aspects of life (*dharma*);
- Earning money by honest means to provide for wife and children (*artha*);
- Enjoying the good things in life by allowing for small 'treats' in daily routine (*kama*);
- Leading the soul towards God to achieve release from successive deaths and births (*moksha*). (Hindus believe in life after death, not just one life but a series of lives, and it is the duty of every person to liberate the soul from this cycle of successive lives.)

The following examples show how two Hindus try to achieve the four aims of life.

An Indian Farmer

Govind is a farmer, who lives in a village with his wife, son, daughter and elderly widowed mother. He also has a grown-up son who works in a factory in a nearby town and sends money every month. Govind starts the day by bathing; this he does in the open by the side of his house. On his way to the fields he visits the temple of the village deity. He celebrates festivals such as Diwali and Holi and takes part in the village fair. He owns some land, and earns his living by working in the fields. He would like to send his younger son to school, but if he does he will have to find someone else to look after the oxen and the buffalo. He does not drink alcohol, but chews tobacco while he is working in the fields. There are very few luxuries in his life, but on festival days his wife prepares sweet, stuffed chapatis (flat bread), and the family enjoys seasonal fruit like mangoes. He can't read or write, but likes to listen to the village teacher, who talks to the villagers in front of the shrine of the deity. He is aware that when he dies, he will be born again somewhere. He offers prayers to the goddess in the shrine to seek her blessing for a good harvest, education for his younger son and a suitable husband for his daughter.

A British Hindu Woman

Gangabai came to Britain with her husband and two daughters after the Second World War. When her husband died five years later, she was left in difficult circumstances with two daughters to feed and educate. She borrowed some money from family friends and bought a small shop. She worked hard to repay the loan, educate her daughters and arrange their marriages. She followed her *dharma* through her hard work.

She kept the shop open very late each evening and gradually it became well-known and popular. Gangabai became a successful businesswoman and when a new Hindu temple was planned, she was able to make a generous donation. When she retired, she spent many hours each day in the temple, helping with the cooking and cleaning and sharing in the prayers.

From these examples, we can see that Hindus from different backgrounds try to achieve their aims in different ways. Religious duty, *dharma*, is given first priority, because all actions in life must be guided by a code of conduct. Hindus are encouraged to enjoy life, fulfil their dreams and desires and then turn their thoughts to the liberation of the soul.

? Discuss how the four *ashramas* help Hindus to keep the balance between spiritual development and social responsibility. How do the four *dharmas* (aims in life) reinforce this?

THE FIVE TYPES OF DAILY WORSHIP (*PANCHA YAJNA*)

Devout Hindu families see daily worship as a religious duty. They carry out this worship by offering water to the wise men who composed the sacred texts, and by making sacrifices to the deities, to the spirits of nature, to the ancestors, and finally to humankind. Worship of the wise is performed first. The sacrifices are then performed by offering cooked rice and clarified butter to the sacred fire kindled in a small copper brazier in the kitchen.

Worship of the Wise (*Brahma Yajna*)

Worshippers repeat and revise everything that they have learned from the holy books, thus remembering the authors who preserved these sacred books for their use. It is not possible to repeat the whole book each time, so one verse from each holy book studied is chanted. Water is offered to the authors of the holy books. This is done by pouring a little cold water on the right hand and allowing it to trickle into a copper dish on the ground. Water is also offered to the gods, earth, oceans, rivers, vegetation and all creatures in the universe. This ritual creates an awareness of the total universe in the mind of the worshipper.

Worship of the Deities (*Deva Yajna*)

Prayers are now offered to Agni, the God of Fire, to carry offerings of rice and clarified butter to the gods. A few grains of rice are dropped in the fire as the names of important deities are uttered. A prayer is said for learning, wealth, good health and long life.

Worship of the Spirits of Nature (*Bhuta Yajna*)

In the same fire, rice is dropped as an offering to the spirits guarding the universe. These include the spirits of water, plants, forests, dwellings and death.

Worship of the Ancestors (*Pitra Yajna*)

A portion of rice and *ghee* (clarified butter) is dropped into the fire as an offering to the spirits of the departed ancestors.

Worship of Humankind (*Manushya Yajna*)

Remembrance of the needy, of visitors and guests is made by dropping one portion of rice in the sacred fire.

The remaining rice on the plate is then taken outside the house into the back garden and placed on a stone for crows and other birds and insects. Worshippers re-enter the house and, standing in front of the fire, say a peace prayer:

> May there be peace on this Earth, and in the Sky. May we get to Heaven. May we become fearless and free from danger. May we have plenty of water, good health and a peaceful life.
>
> Daily *mantra* used by Pandit Narahari,
> the author's family priest; translated by the author.

Though worship is still performed by many devout Hindus in rural India before the midday meal, in large cities and in Western countries where people have neither time nor space to spare, the Gayatri hymn (see Chapter 3) may be repeated five times in place of this worship. If uninvited guests call just before the meal, they are to be welcomed and fed.

DONATION OR GIFT (*DANA*)

Various books on the practice of *dharma* encourage Hindus to give gifts on specific festival days to gain religious merit. The Bhagavad-Gita, a Hindu holy book, describes the types of gifts and the merit they bestow on the giver:

> The highest merit is bestowed by that gift which is given as a duty to a worthy person at the right time, with no expectation of any return or benefit.
>
> A gift given reluctantly or while expecting something in return will attract only a fair religious merit.
>
> A gift given to an unworthy person at the wrong time and place, without respect or with an insult, brings very little merit to the giver.
>
> Bhagavad-Gita, Chapter 17, verses 20–2.

If a gift or donation is given as a religious act, then it should be given at a holy place where devout people gather. The rules quoted above do not prevent anyone giving to the poor and the needy; the poor and needy are always considered worthy and the time and place is here and now.

<table>
<tr><td>

Chapter

6

</td><td>

The Influence of Hinduism in India and Britain

</td></tr>
</table>

HINDUISM IN INDIA

Many airlines have daily flights to Delhi or Bombay and will fly you to India in nine hours. If you leave Heathrow Airport in London in the afternoon, your plane will land at Bombay International Airport early the next morning. As you walk through the 'green channel' at customs, you will see many Indian passengers being met by their relatives. Many of them will be Hindus; they will exchange Hindu greetings by joining their palms in front of them and saying the words *namaste* or *namaskar*.

When you get into a taxi to go to your hotel, you are likely to see a photograph of a Hindu holy man on the dashboard. The driver will have placed a flower garland round the picture and lit an incense-stick in prayer to the holy man to bring good business that day.

As your taxi travels to your hotel, you will see the city coming to life; the shops open when the pavement in front has been swept and sprinkled with water; women wearing saris and older men wearing *dhotis* set out on their way to work, even though it is only about four o'clock in the morning.

Visitors to the Laxmi-Narayan temple in Delhi. This modern temple is often referred to as the Birla temple since the founding donation was given by the famous Indian industrialist G.D. Birla.

Later on, you will see the shop signboards written in Hindi script, and some which are still painted in English. A number of cafés have vegetarian food, and the sweetmeat shops sell typical Hindu sweets.

Outside the large temples in Bombay you will see coconuts, flowers, incense-sticks and flower garlands for sale. After an early bath some Hindus visit the temples to offer flowers and prayers. The younger women wear very colourful saris, and Westernised young men wear cotton shirts and trousers. Both men and women wear a red mark (a *tilak*) on their foreheads as they come out of the temple.

If you travelled to a small town not far from Bombay, you would notice similar activities going on. Early bathing, prayers at the household shrine and a visit to a temple are even more common in the smaller towns and villages of India. If the town is near a river, there will be many temples of different sizes dedicated to various gods such as Vishnu, Rama, Krishna, Ganesha, Hanuman and the goddess Parvati – all of them different forms of the One God which Hindus worship.

If you went to a village, you would see most of the men and women wearing *dhotis* and saris. The small temple or shrine would be of a deity which protects the villagers.

Festivals

The most noticeable influence of Hinduism in India is seen in the celebration of festivals, whether of an all-India appeal such as Diwali or Holi, or only of local interest such as Durga Puja or the Ganesha festival. These festivals are celebrated with music, dancing, singing and processions, and the whole community is involved. The same applies to the celebration of life-cycle rituals, *samskaras*, such as initiation, marriage and funeral.

Holy Books

Hinduism has many holy books. The oldest are the Vedas and the Upanishads, which deal with philosophy and the idea of life after death. They also put forward the difficult concept of *karma*: the result of each person's actions throughout life which decides the form in which each person will be reborn. The epic stories, the Mahabharata and the Ramayana, the Hindu legends and the Bhagavad-Gita are more popular holy books. These scriptures have all influenced Hindu thought and the way in which God is worshipped all over Hindu India. Villagers are familiar with the Rama story, although they cannot read the ancient language, Sanskrit, in which the story is written, and priests in many temples in towns and villages retell the various legends at the time of festivals. The Hindu scriptures are dealt with more fully in Chapters 10, 11 and 12.

Social Divisions

Perhaps the greatest influence of Hinduism in India is seen in the *varna* classification into which Hindu society is divided (see Chapter 5). Associated with the *varna* classification is another one based on birth and occupation, known as the 'caste system'. (Chapter 13 gives a more detailed description of the caste system.)

The influence of the Hindu caste system is gradually diminishing, but caste is still important, both in India and elsewhere, when arranging marriages, and, in some cases, when applying for a good job.

Admittedly there are many people in India who are not Hindus, but, since 80 per cent are, it is the Hindu influence in everyday life that is the most visible and obvious nearly everywhere. The influence of the caste system has spread to other, non-Hindu, communities in India; and the extended family, though the result of the Hindu idea of group loyalty and religious duty, is common throughout India.

? How would a visitor to India come to the conclusion that it was a more religious country than Britain? Would they necessarily be correct?

HINDUISM IN BRITAIN

In 1987 it was estimated that there were 350 000 Hindus living and working in Britain, though the influence and practice of Hinduism in Britain is of recent origin. It is not possible to identify Hindus in Britain by observing them superficially – an Asian-looking person will not necessarily be a Hindu, and, though many Hindu women wear saris, so too do Muslims and Christians, while some Hindu women and most Hindu men wear European clothes! On a closer examination, you might notice a red mark on a person's forehead – this person would be a Hindu. Personal names, too, can help identify a Hindu. Most of all, though, you would be able to identify Hindus from the way they worship God.

As we have seen, there is no standard form of Hindu worship or of celebrating festivals and rites of passage even in India, because of the regional variations in language, food, climate and local customs. Likewise in Britain, although the particular form and experience of the faith is part of the larger tradition of Hinduism, worship patterns have changed to suit local circumstances.

A large majority of British Hindus originate from the Punjab and from Gujarat, and may have come to Britain via East Africa where they were born. Smaller numbers come from other regions of India, while many Hindus were born in Britain and are British citizens by birth. The term 'British Hindu' denotes both nationality and cultural background.

Hindu Communities and Temples

A number of Hindu communities, each based on knowledge of a common language, such as Gujarati, Punjabi or Tamil, have established themselves in different cities in Britain. By far the largest number are in the Greater London area and the Midlands, but fewer Hindus have settled in Scotland or the cities and towns on the south coast. In Bradford, temples dedicated to deities such as Vishnu or his *avatars* (incarnations), Rama and Krishna, and to the goddess Parvati, are run by Gujarati- or Punjabi-speaking Hindus. The worshippers follow the mainstream form of Hinduism, which they refer to as the *Sanatana-dharma*.

Plan of the hall of a Hindu temple in Britain. Worshippers sit facing each other, between the deities and the priest.

There are also Hindu temples in Preston, Leicester, Loughborough, Birmingham, Coventry, Wolverhampton and other cities in the Midlands, as well as in Southall, Leyton and Golders Green in London. Most of these temples are housed in buildings of familiar British design and do not stand out as unusual landmarks. Many temples conduct classes in Indian languages, music, dance and cookery, since Hindu temples in Britain serve as places of worship as well as community centres.

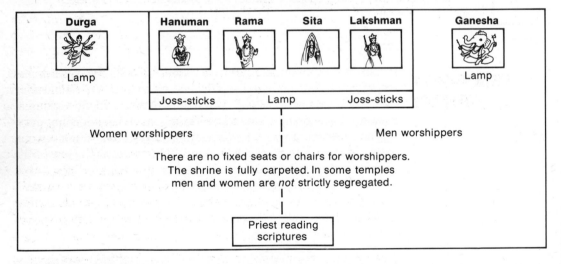

VARIETIES OF HINDUISM

The practice of Hinduism varies and an individual is allowed total freedom of choice of a personal deity or a human guru, of the method of worship and of the performance of rituals. Some Hindus follow particular movements, in which they offer worship to a living guru or teacher in order to receive guidance in this life and to attain liberation of the soul after death. In some of these movements the human teacher, usually the head of the organisation, is worshipped instead of an image of a deity, although in others a deity is also worshipped. The teacher is expected to be learned and to be an example to his followers. The followers receive a *mantra* (sacred verse) from their teacher or guru, to repeat during meditation.

The Sathya Sai Baba Movement

This movement, in which disciples worship and seek guidance from a living guru, was started in Britain by a small number of Hindus in 1966. The guru, Sathya Sai Baba, was born in India in 1926, exactly eight years after the death of an earlier teacher, Shirdi Sai Baba (1868–1918). Shirdi Sai Baba claimed that he was an incarnation of Kabir, a poet-saint who lived in the fifteenth century; he was claimed by Hindus to be a Hindu and by Muslims to be a Muslim. From the age of 14, Sathya Sai Baba was considered to be an incarnation of Shirdi Sai Baba by a large number of his followers. The present guru, who lives in India, uses Hindu forms of expression, but admits that other religions are valid paths to God. Disciples in Britain usually meet for *bhajans* (singing devotional songs), offer worship to a photograph of the guru and lead their lives according to five principles. These principles are *satya* (truth), *dharma* (righteous conduct), *shanti* (peace), *prema* (love) and *ahimsa* (non-injury).

A temple shrine in London dedicated to Sai Baba of Shirdi.

The Hare Krishna Movement

The International Society for Krishna Consciousness (ISKCON) was first started in America by a Hindu who based his teachings on an earlier Hindu tradition of the worship of Vishnu. Within the Hare Krishna movement the worship of Krishna is preached and practised, although the founder-guru, Bhaktivedanta, and the heads of various centres are very important and guide their followers according to a strict code of belief and practice.

The first Hare Krishna temple in London was opened in 1969. The organisers managed to get a lot of publicity in the press and hoped to attract British Hindus to their movement. Swami Bhaktivedanta came to London to instal the images of Krishna and Radha. The temple distributed *prasad* and introduced a high level of ritual worship, which gradually attracted young British Hindus to the movement. They had never seen this elaborate ritual, since their parents merely performed a simple *puja* at the household shrine.

Hare Krishna followers are strict vegetarians. In the residential temple near Watford, men and women devotees have separate living quarters, and the use of tobacco, drugs and alcohol is strictly prohibited. The followers of this form of Hinduism are easily identified by their orange coloured clothes, and by the shaven heads of the men.

Many Westerners have joined the Hare Krishna movement. What do you think attracts young people to it? When you have discussed this, it may be possible to invite some Hare Krishna members to school so that you can discover their reasons and they can discuss your findings. They could also tell you about their lifestyle.

Arya Samaj

This movement has two centres in the London area, in Chalk Farm and in Ealing, where the members of the Arya Samaj (Society of Aryans) meet regularly, usually to offer worship to the sacred fire. Arya Samaj was founded in north India in the late nineteenth century by Swami Dayananda, as a reformed version of Hinduism. The members of Arya Samaj hold the Vedas to be both sacred and supreme, but reject later developments in Hinduism, such as the worship of images as symbols of the Highest God. They do, however, use the sacred symbol *Aum* to represent the Supreme Spirit, *Brahman*, and worship the sacred fire by offering grain and *ghee* while chanting passages from the Vedas. The weekly gatherings are called *satsang*, an assembly of the pious, and freshly cooked food is shared by everyone present. This practice is important, since it helps to break down the traditional caste barriers; the Arya Samaj considers all members equal and there is no human guru as the head of their place of worship. The Arya Samaj is described in more detail in Chapter 16.

Swami Narayan Movement

This new form of Hinduism was founded by Sahajananda Swami in the early nineteenth century in Gujarat, India, and it was open to all sections of society. The followers of the Swami declared him to be Swami Narayan, a divine embodiment of Narayan, another name for Vishnu. He was believed to be capable of granting salvation to his followers. The movement has grown considerably since the 1820s and there are many self-governing branches in India and Britain. In the UK, members of the movement belong to the well-to-do Gujarati merchant group, most of whom came to Britain from East Africa.

His Divine Holiness Shree Pramukh Swami, head of the Swami Narayan movement; he is considered to be an incarnation of Narayan, and to be capable of granting liberation from samsara. *As a living God, he is always offered worship first, before other deities.*

A visit to a Swaminarayan temple

The temple is within the Swaminarayan complex near Neasden, north London. The Rama-Navami day, Rama's birthday, is also the birthday of the founder, Swami Narayan, so there was a double celebration. The main temple and other rooms are fully carpeted and spotlessly clean. The shrine containing pictures of Swami Narayan, along with those of Radha and Krishna and Laxmi-Narayan, is at one end of the main hall, which can seat over 3000 people. Men and women sit separately. Large quantities of Indian sweets were neatly arranged in front of the shrine, as offerings from the devotees; there was sufficient for distribution as *prasad* to at least 2000 people.

For Rama's birthday celebrations, two swinging cots bearing Rama's pictures were placed on either side of the food offering, so that all the devotees were able to view at least one cot. The Rama story was narrated in Gujarati, and then a member of the managing committee recounted Swami Narayan's life and work. *Arati* was performed with at least six *arati* trays; musical accompaniment was provided by a harmonium, tabla drums and small brass cymbals. When the *arati* lights were taken among the congregation, people received the holy light with their hands and made generous money offerings. I was permitted by the chairman and the members of the managing committee to speak to the congregation about the teaching of Hinduism in British schools and about the relevance of their experience as Hindus.

A member of the committee then showed me other parts of the building, which are used as a library, administrative offices, medical screening room and a recording room where devotional music is recorded on tapes and sold to the devotees. The youth centre is attended by about 500 children each week to learn Gujarati and the central beliefs of the Swaminarayan religion. Floor-to-ceiling racks are neatly arranged to the left of the entrance to the temple hall, where visitors may remove and store their shoes.

Every person in the large congregation was served with a mouthwatering meal as *prasad*. The bookstall on the way out sold publications in Gujarati and English, and a large body of dedicated volunteers guarded the vehicles in the car park.

The Swaminarayan religion has a congregational form of worship and the emphasis is on moral duty (*dharma*), as well as earning money (*artha*) and enjoying the good things of life (*kama*), which shows the positive attitude essential for a successful life. In Britain, the followers are hard-working and law-abiding Hindus, involved in community care and a great deal of charitable work.

Shiva, Parvati, Ganesha and Krishna are the chief deities worshipped. The followers believe in the theory of *karma* and rebirth, and celebrate important Hindu festivals and many life-cycle rites with much enthusiasm.

1 Some Hindus believe it is only possible to be a Hindu by being born one. What reasons might they give for this attitude?

2 Create a discussion between a convert to Hinduism (perhaps through the Hare Krishna movement) and someone who says that to be a Hindu one must be born a Hindu.

Chapter 7

Expression of Belief in Daily Life

Hindus express their belief in God in a variety of ways in daily life and worship. Some of these are described in Chapter 1. This chapter looks at five important religious paths or ways of expressing belief and approaching God in worship and understanding. Each individual may choose the path(s) most appropriate to his or her nature and abilities.

THE PATH OF *BHAKTI* (DEVOTION)

The path of devotion is the simplest way for most Hindus to experience the One-ness that exists between the individual spirit, *atman*, and the Universal Spirit, *Brahman*. On a high philosophical level, *Brahman* is without form – a difficult concept for the ordinary worshipper to understand. The follower of *bhakti* therefore centres devotion on a personal God (*ishwara*) of his or her choice; this deity may be Laxmi, Shiva, Krishna, Rama or any other of the Hindu deities. An image of the chosen deity is used to help concentrate the thoughts of those following the path of devotion. The personal deity, or *ishwara*, represents an aspect of the Supreme Spirit, *Brahman*.

The way of *bhakti* (devotion) firstly requires a firm belief in a personal God of love and mercy and a single-minded love for that deity. The worshipper has complete faith and trust in God and makes a total surrender to the will of God. It is believed that God will keep safe all who are devoted to Him.

Marble images of Krishna and Radha, dressed for worship, in a north London temple.

Hindus who follow the path of devotion practise four actions which enable them to form a close relationship with their *ishwara*:

- they delight in hearing the praises of God;
- they bow low before the image of God and chant His name;
- they try to remember Him at all times;
- they serve the deity by offering daily worship and serve others by doing good deeds in His name.

The way of devotion does not find knowledge of God through books or meditation; no specific rituals are required; and no barriers of class or occupation divide the worshipper from his or her God. Only an emotional awareness of God and constant remembrance of him are necessary. The whole life should be a sacrifice to God. As Lord Krishna says in the Bhagavad-Gita:

Whatever you do, eat, offer as an oblation,
give as a gift or undertake as a penance,
offer all that to Me, O Arjuna.

The ultimate goal of this devotion is to be near God or to let the individual spirit merge into the spirit of God. This state is perfect joy, and the soul will never be reborn again but remain in one-ness with God for ever.

THE PATH OF KARMA (ACTION)

The word *karma* has two meanings: action, e.g. all physical activities, such as walking, eating, speaking, sleeping and all thought processes, both good and evil; and the total effect of one's actions. The result of the action attaches to the individual spirit, *atman*, and the consequences of action force the individual spirit to remain tied to the cycle of birth, death and rebirth and determine what form its next existence will take. A Hindu's final goal is to achieve freedom from this cycle of birth, death and rebirth; and to reach that goal the result of one's actions, one's *karma*, must not bind the spirit.

No human being can go through life without normal physical and mental activity; care must be taken to do actions that will have a good effect. A life full of selfless activity is the correct way of using God-given talents and reaching full potential; it is not good to abandon action for fear of bad results. The path of *karma* thus benefits society as well as the individual, and doing one's job to the best of one's ability is the readiest way of serving God.

THE PATH OF JNANA (KNOWLEDGE)

The path of knowledge is the most difficult, since the follower of this path must have a learned teacher, and very few people have the ability to understand the complicated ideas expressed in the Vedas and the Upanishads. These scriptures deal with the idea of the Supreme Spirit, *Brahman*; the individual spirit, *atman*; the nature of the universe and man's place in it. Through a clear understanding of the scriptures, people are able to free themselves from the bonds of attachment that bind them to the material world. Only when they have freed themselves from the material world are they able to reach the higher spiritual level.

THE PATH OF YOGA

The word *yoga* comes from a Sanskrit verb meaning 'to join'. Yoga joins the spiritual forces of the mind to the material forces of the body, so that both work together as a controlled unit. A successful follower of yoga can release hidden energy in his or her body, which leads to greater control of life. This, in turn, gives rise to health, long life and peace of mind. Yoga is a path which leads to the liberation of the individual spirit from the cycle of successive lives. There are three different kinds of yoga:

Dr Anuragi, formerly a member of the Nimbaraka sect, but now a follower of Mahesh Yogi. He and his followers wear the mark of Vishnu on their foreheads. The sacred thread is worn by the elderly disciple seated on the right.

Hatha Yoga

This yoga uses various exercises and postures to achieve bodily control. Such yoga exercises and breath control must be learned under the supervision of an expert teacher to avoid harm and injury.

Dhyana Yoga

This yoga concentrates on meditation, as a result of which the soul (the individual spirit) is made more aware of its one-ness with the Supreme Spirit, *Brahman*.

Raja Yoga

This yoga lays stress on spiritual discipline rather than on physical exercises. This highest form of yoga is called the 'King of Kings' yoga; it needs no external forms or techniques. It involves deep contemplation of *Brahman* and, when success is achieved, the mind is freed from anger, lust, fear, greed, envy and sadness.

AHIMSA

In Sanskrit *himsa* means 'killing' or 'injury', and *ahimsa* means 'non-killing' or 'non-injury'. *Ahimsa* is an important virtue of Hindu ethics, along with truth and honesty. *Ahimsa* expresses the sanctity of all forms of life: insects, fish, birds, animals and human beings. In order to practise *ahimsa*, it is necessary to give up all actions which lead to the taking of life or the shedding of blood, and to avoid eating all animal flesh. Ideally, all physical, mental, emotional or moral hurt to any living thing must be avoided.

The Hindu practice of *ahimsa* is determined by two factors. First, the meaning of the word is normally accepted to be 'non-injury', which is a negative concept and lacks the positive force of the Christian Commandment, 'Thou shalt love the Lord thy God and thy neighbour as thyself.' It is enough for Hindus to avoid harm to others. They don't think it is their duty to interfere to prevent such harm being caused by other people. This negative approach results in indifference to what others are doing.

Secondly, Hindus restrict the meaning of *ahimsa* to 'non-killing' or 'not shedding blood', and ignore other forms of hurt such as pain and suffering through lack of food and medical attention, the mental anguish experienced by those condemned to doing dirty jobs all

The cart-puller, more fortunate than many, rests, while the driver gets to work . . .

. . . but the animals here have to rely on rubbish dumps for most of their food.

their lives, the degradation suffered by millions who sleep on the pavements in large cities like Bombay, Calcutta or Madras, leading a 'hand to mouth' existence, and the pain and suffering experienced by domestic and working animals through lack of proper food and shelter. The reason put forward as a defence for this indifference is that if a creature is suffering pain or degradation it is the result of *karma* in a previous life, and no human interference can lessen that pain. In other words, the pain is *earned* by the suffering creature, whether an animal or a human being.

The Suffering of Other Creatures

It is true that a tiny minority of Westernised Hindus living in affluent parts of large cities do have house pets and care for them very sincerely. But the vast majority of Hindus show indifference to the mental, emotional and moral hurts of other creatures and permit the *himsa* (hurt) caused by pain and suffering, and by lack of food, medical care, shelter and dignity of life, to continue.

Some foreign travellers in the sixteenth century have left written accounts of hospitals for animals, which they visited in India at that time. Even today there are 'hostels' for sick or infirm animals, where they are allowed to die naturally but without the help of medical intervention, such as pain-killing drugs. This lack of compassion for unfortunate humans and animals cannot be easily reconciled with the noble principle of Hinduism: the individual spirit within every creature is a part of the Universal Spirit.

Passive Resistance

During the struggle for Indian Independence from the British Raj, Mahatma Gandhi applied the principle of *ahimsa* to his civil disobedience and passive resistance movement. It was supposed to be non-violent resistance to British political authority in India, and Gandhi's followers were not armed. The police, however, were forced to use their long sticks to beat the large numbers of freedom fighters, many of whom were injured, and many more were put in jail. The movement based on *ahimsa* in fact resulted in a great deal of violence.

Mahatma Gandhi with his followers during his civil disobedience campaign against the salt monopoly in 1930. His life followed the path of karma *(action), and wherever he was, he showed concern for the underprivileged and the suffering (see also Chapter 16).*

1   Hindus often describe their religion as 'many paths leading to one goal'. What do you think they mean by this?
2   Hindus are often encouraged to follow the path best suited to them. Make a table with four columns, one for each path, and make lists of kinds of people and the path which might suit them best.
3   Discuss which path might be most suitable for (a) a lonely person; (b) someone who enjoys parties and crowds; (c) a reflective person; and (d) a kind and caring person.

<table>
<tr><td>Chapter
8</td><td><h1>Deities in Indian Villages</h1></td></tr>
</table>

A very large percentage of the Hindu population of India live in the villages. As we have seen, the practice of Hinduism differs widely in different regions because of language, food, climatic variation, local customs and family traditions; and, outside India, the practice of the faith is modified to suit conditions in various parts of the world. The urban, middle-class variety of Hinduism is quite different from the faith practised in the villages of India and, even here, there is little uniformity since the composition of every village is different. There is, however, enough similarity from village to village for us to be able to talk of 'village Hinduism' or 'popular Hinduism'. The following account gives an insight into the Hinduism of one village.

A Village Headman and his Nephew

During my recent visit to India I went to a village near my town and spoke to the headman, a farmer, and his nephew, a primary school teacher about 25 years old.

'Ram-Ram, Patil,' I greeted him, using the usual form of address showing respect for his position in the village.
'Ram-Ram,' he replied, 'where are you from?'
'I live in Wilayat (England) and work as a teacher there.'

A small Bheru temple by the roadside in a north Indian village.

'My brother's son is also a teacher,' he proudly informed me, and introduced me to his nephew. He gave me a handful of peanuts as a gesture of welcome and, later, a cup of tea, as we sat outside his house.

'Is that a Shiva temple in the square?' I asked.

'No,' he replied. 'That god is called Bheru.'

'Sometimes', said the nephew, 'he is called Bhairav.'

'But there is a stone bull in front of the temple. The god must be Shiva,' I pointed out.

'There is a stone bull, yes, but Bheru is not Shiva. The Shiva temple is near the river and only the Brahmin priest goes there. We never visit that temple or the Ganapati (Ganesha) temple.' He spoke with conviction.

'Why don't you visit those temples?' I asked.

'Because Shiva and Ganapati don't look after us,' replied the nephew.

'But, Patil,' I said, 'Bheru, Shiva and Ganapati are different names of One Bhagwan.'

'Well,' replied the headman, 'yes, they are. But Bhagwan is too busy to find time for villagers like us, and Shiva and Ganapati are really Brahmin Gods. So we go to Bheru and make our simple *puja*, because He understands our problems. We hold a *jatra* (fair) every year for Bheru and Mata.'

'Is Mata Bheru's wife?' I asked.

'No,' replied the nephew. 'Mata is our "Mother". She is a *devi* (goddess). In the villages around us she is also called Ma, Amma, Ai and Mari-Ai. She looks after the whole village, all people including the Brahmin priest. Her temple is not as large as the Bheru temple, but in some ways she is more important.'

'In what way?' I asked.

'She will bring us good luck if we regularly visit the temple and give her things.'

'What sort of things, Patil?'

'Well, . . . flowers, or a coconut . . . and at the time of *jatra*, a chicken.'

'What happens if you don't give her these things?'

'Everything begins to go wrong. Someone becomes ill, the buffalo stops giving milk, and sometimes the crops are poor.'

'And Mata looks after the babies too,' said the nephew. 'All babies have to be taken to the Mata temple on their first outing. Even the Brahmin priest took his two babies to the Mata temple.'

'There is another *devi* called Sitala,' said Patil. 'She protects all people in the village from smallpox.'

'When things go right,' said the nephew, 'when the rains come on time, when the crops are good, we give a red cloth to Mata to show how grateful we are.'

'Are there any other *devis* that look after the village?' I asked.

'Yes, but they don't have any temples,' replied the nephew. 'Some are good spirits and they bring us benefits, others are bad ones and they sometimes cause trouble. All village people believe that these *devis* reside at the crossroads, on the pipal tree, on the hilltop nearby and in the bamboo thicket at the edge of the village.'

'How do they cause trouble?' I asked.

'Sometimes a child becomes ill for no reason. Then we think it is suffering from someone's *najar* (eye of envy) – maybe the spirit of a dead woman who had no children.'

'What do people do when that happens?'

'Well, the parents of the child put some cooked rice on a banana leaf and put it on a stone at the crossroads. The child soon recovers.'

Women making offerings to the sacred stones near a village temple during the annual Devi-puja.

'What does the spirit at the edge of the village do?' I asked.

'She protects us from outsiders. We leave some chapatis and vegetable curry there every full moon.'

'Patil, you said that Shiva and Ganapati were Brahmin Gods,' I continued, 'but Brahmins also worship Hanuman. Do you worship Hanuman?'

'Really Hanuman is a village god, because all wrestlers worship him. Also you must have seen a stone, painted red, at the foot of the large pipal tree! That stone is the tree-spirit. When we go past the tree, we put some of the red colour from the stone on our foreheads as *tika*, to bring us good luck.'

After spending an hour talking to old Patil, the village headman, and his nephew, I thanked them for tea and made my way back to town. As I walked past the large pipal tree, I also put some red colour from the stone on my forehead for luck.

GRAMA-DEVATAS

Each village in India is protected by its own set of guardian deities or *gramadevatas*. These are the lesser deities of Hinduism, who are more accessible to the villagers and who, the villagers believe, can help solve their problems.

From the account above, we see that *Brahman*, the Highest God in Hinduism, is referred to by the villagers as 'Bhagwan'. He is too great for the ordinary villager to understand fully, just as the major gods and goddesses, such as Vishnu, Shiva, Laxmi, Parvati, Ganesha and Hanuman, whom the villagers call *devis* (goddesses) or *devas* (gods), are too remote for them to approach meaningfully.

The villagers therefore turn to the *gramadevatas*, who are more real, more accessible, and more important to them.

A DIFFERENT FAITH?

Some scholars hold that village Hinduism is a completely different faith; others think that it is only in the villages that the entire range of belief and practice of Hinduism can be seen.

1   Explain to a visitor to your Indian village, perhaps from another country, how you are helped by believing that there are specific gods who look after your village.

2   What reasons can be put forward for suggesting that village Hinduism is a very different faith from the *Sanatana-dharma*?
    How might a Brahmin in a village argue in order to reject the view?

Part II

Historical Perspective

Chapter 9

The Beginnings of Hinduism

As we noted at the beginning of this book, the word 'Hindu' was used by the ancient Persians to refer to the people who lived on the other side of the river Indus. Who were these people and what relevance do they have to the faith that we know today as Hinduism? This section of the book attempts to answer these questions and to chart the development of Hinduism from its very early beginnings, through its literature and scriptures, to the way it is practised today.

THE INDUS VALLEY PEOPLE

For a long time very little was known about the Indus Valley people. The remains dug up during the 1920s at various sites in the valley, particularly at the sites of the two walled cities, Mohenjo-daro and Harappa, now in Pakistan, have proved the existence of a great river civilisation, which flourished between 3000 and 2000 BCE, and have helped answer some baffling questions about early civilisation in India.

Recent excavations by French archaeologists have unearthed sites of two further cities at Mehrgarh and Naushahro in western Pakistan, which suggests that the Indus Valley civilisation may be even older, being at its height in 6000 BCE. Even at that time pottery figures of women and bulls were produced, and 1500 years later painted ceramics were common.

The Indus Script

The Indus people had a form of writing, found on various seals dug up at the sites, measuring 3–4 cm square. Unfortunately, nobody has yet been able to decode the script. And so, in the absence of written documents, all our information about the Indus river civilisation is based on excavated remains over 4000 years old.

The Indus Civilisation

Indus Valley seals.

From the extent of the sites it is believed that the Indus civilisation covered an area larger than Egypt or Mesopotamia, and was equally advanced in culture and in the use of tools. No iron has been discovered, but copper and bronze were widely in use. From the dug-up sites we see that the chief towns were planned with care and divided into zones with wide streets running due east–west and north–south. The drainage system had pottery drainpipes and covered sewers. Rainwater and waste water from the houses was carefully channelled.

The buildings had flat roofs, no ornamentations, and were of large burnt or sun-dried bricks. The houses had many rooms, windows and open courtyards, and the large buildings with pillared rooms were probably assembly halls. We know that the Indus Valley people were skilled metal-workers, since bronze statues, jewellery, copper beakers and tools have been found. Highly glazed and decorated pottery has been unearthed in large quantities at various sites. Small figures in soapstone, clay or limestone, as well as children's toys shaped like birds and animals, have been found, which suggests that life was peaceful and children had time to play.

The clothes worn by the Indus people were similar to those worn by the inhabitants of Sumer and Egypt; a loincloth and a shawl for the upper body, with a form of turban for the head. We know that both men and women wore jewellery, because many necklaces of gold and semi-precious stone beads have been found. The Indus people cultivated wheat and barley, and their diet included meat and fish.

Religion

Unfortunately we know little about the religion of these people, since the only written evidence we have comes from the seals which are so far undeciphered. The excavations show ruins of large ceremonial buildings and public baths, which indicate that the Indus people appear to have placed great emphasis on religious or ritual purification. Remains of masks and distinctive head-dresses give evidence of a priesthood, and we know that certain life-cycle rituals such as funerals were given serious attention and concern. It is likely that the people of Mohenjo-daro cremated their dead, since no cemetery has been found there; whilst at Harappa, burial was the normal rite after death and burials were carried out elaborately.

Excavation of the Great Bath, Mohenjo-daro.

From the evidence of female figurines, it seems that there was a strong emphasis on fertility in religious belief and worship. One seal shows a female figure nursing a small child, which may represent a mother goddess. On another seal a goddess is shown waiting for an animal to be sacrificed before her. Scholars believe that this goddess was adopted by the invading Aryans and later developed into the Hindu Durga or Kali.

A male deity sitting cross-legged and surrounded by animals probably became the Hindu Shiva. On some seals the deity has a crescent moon on his head, or has three faces. These details show a connection with various later names of Shiva, such as 'Moon-Crested', 'Three-Faced', 'Lord of Beasts' and 'Great Yogi'. The typical cross-legged yoga posture of the deity shows the Indian meditation pose and suggests that yoga exercises, meditation and philosophy are pre-Aryan in origin.

The animals found on the seals are an ox-like beast with a single horn, a humped bull, a rhinoceros, a tiger, an antelope, a fish-eating crocodile and an eagle carrying a snake.

Look at the pictures of the Indus seals on page 62. Their meaning and purpose are still unknown, but, if they are religious, what kinds of beliefs do you think their owners might have had?

THE ARYAN INVADERS

At first it was assumed that the invading Aryans, who came into India from somewhere in north central Asia in about 1500 BCE, destroyed the Indus cities and absorbed the inhabitants into Aryan society by force. This view has since been modified by some scholars who suggest that the Indus civilisation was already in decline when the Aryans came into contact with it. Changes in the course of the river caused some cities to be destroyed by floods, and Mohenjo-daro seems to have been re-built many times. Scholars believe that it was finally destroyed by either a severe flood, climatic change or an epidemic.

The Aryan newcomers certainly adopted many material things and philosophical ideas from the Indus people and over many centuries made them completely Aryan. Who were these Aryans? Where did they live before they migrated into India in about 1500 BCE? Did they settle somewhere for a time before finally entering India?

Who were the Aryans?

The Aryans are a family of peoples, also known as the Indo-Europeans. The word 'arya', still used in India, means noble, and it was applied by the Aryans to themselves. The name 'Iran', too, is derived from 'Aryan'. The most commonly held view among scholars is that the Aryans came from the steppes of Russia and central Asia in about 2000 BCE. One group travelled into Europe, while the other spread through Asia Minor into Iran. It is possible that the Aryans who entered India in about 1500 BCE were a branch of the Iranian group.

The Aryans were tall, fair-skinned and light-eyed. Originally they were nomadic cattle herdsmen and hunters, but they soon became farmers when they settled in India. They were an aggressive people and extended their sway through conquest and colonisation, but they were less civilised than the original inhabitants of India, who were dark-skinned and smaller in build.

The Vedic Aryans worshipped deities who controlled the forces of nature and they spoke a distinctive Aryan language. They domesticated the horse and the cow and used tools of iron, copper and bronze. The ancient Hindu scripture known as the Veda contains the faith and customs of the Indian branch of the Aryans, and the period of development of early Aryan culture in India is called the Vedic period.

The Religion of the Aryans

We have no definite knowledge of the religion of the Indus people, but, in the case of the Vedic Aryans, we have a wealth of information on their beliefs and religious practices. The Vedas (books of knowledge) of the Aryans depict these beliefs and practices as they existed about the period 1000 BCE, some time after the Aryans had begun to settle in India. The early hymns of the Rig-Veda (the first and most important of the four books of the Vedas) are about nature: about the sun, rivers, oceans, hills, daybreak and the 'soft, white milk given by the rough red cow' – there is no reference to the mysteries of life and death.

The early Vedic religion was simple nature-worship. There were neither temples nor images, and the 'place of sacrifice' could be laid out anywhere. The gods were invoked by singing hymns inviting them to attend the sacrifices, and they were assumed to be present during the rites. Priests preserved the tribal history, legends and hymns, and handed them down to the next generation by word of mouth; they also helped the chieftains and householders in the performance of the rites. The gods were flattered through prayer in order to gain favour.

Many deities are praised in the Vedas. Some of them, which show the Aryan concern with the natural forces and the family, are:

- Indra, the Lord of Heaven
- Aditi, a mother goddess
- the *Adityas* (children of Aditi)
- Agni, the God of Fire
- Aryaman, the God of Dead Ancestors

- the *Maruts*, Gods of Storm
- Mitra, the God of Light
- Parjanya, a deity of rain
- Prithivi, the Earth Goddess
- Rudra, Chief of the Storm Deities
- Surya, the Sun God
- Varuna, the Lord of the Waters
- Yama, the God of Death

An ideal life in the Vedic age included the practice of virtues such as giving to charity, self-restraint, duty and valour in battle. A virtuous life was rewarded by a place in heaven, but those who failed to practise these virtues were sent to a dark abyss. The dead were either buried or burned.

Aryan Society

The Vedic Aryans loved the good things of life. They ate meat, and bulls were sacrificed and eaten on special occasions. They drank intoxicating drinks and loved hunting, gambling, dancing and music. Vedic society was organised on a tribal basis, each tribe headed by a chieftain and consisting of a number of related families, the father being the head of each family. The hymn called the Purusha Sukta in the Rig-Veda (see Chapter 10) explains how the tribes were organised into groups according to merit and to the jobs they did, though these *varna* divisions were not rigid.

Men married one wife at a time. Women in general, and wives in particular, received great honour, shared with their husbands the duties of performing sacrifices, and took all the domestic decisions. The Rig-Veda makes no mention of child marriage or the prohibition of remarriage of widows.

Imagine you live in one of the Indus cities. Explain your beliefs and practices in a discussion with an Aryan who tells you about his.

THE MIXING OF THE TWO CULTURES

The performance of sacrifices to please the gods was a widely practised ritual of the Vedic people in the early centuries of their stay in their new land. But, through their contact with the original civilisation in the Indus Valley, the Aryans gradually adopted the 'Mother Goddess' cult and the male deity of the Indus Valley people, who was later to become Shiva. The deities of present-day Hinduism reflect both the mother goddess devotion of the Indus Valley people and the predominantly male concepts of God of the invading Aryans.

It is probable that the idea of ritual purity among the Indus people may have been adopted by the Aryans as they settled in their new land, intermarried with the original inhabitants and gradually extended their sway eastwards. The earlier civilisation greatly influenced developing Aryan culture, and by 1000 BCE the Aryan tradition was firmly established in north India. Conversely, the Aryans seem to have influenced and absorbed the Indus people and other groups, because by the fourth century BCE a very large part of India, all except the extreme south, was ruled by Aryan kings of the Maurya dynasty.

?

Some of the distinctive features of Hinduism are:
- the caste system,
- the Vedas,
- ritual purity,
- female deities, often as the consorts of male deities such as Krishna or Shiva,
- asceticism,
- vegetarianism (though not all Hindus are vegetarians),
- ritual bathing,
- yoga,
- cremation of the dead

Which of these may have Indus Valley origins? Which seem to be Aryan? Can you suggest some reasons why the religion of the Aryans did not totally replace the religion of the original inhabitants of India, even though the Aryans became the rulers?

<table>
<tr><td></td><td></td></tr>
</table>

Chapter 10

The First Hindu Scriptures

SHRUTI TEXTS

The ancient Aryans began composing their religious texts about 3500 years ago. The compositions were not written down, but were learned off by heart and passed on to the next generation by word of mouth, from teacher to pupil. The earliest Hindu scriptures, amongst them the Vedas (see below), are *shruti* texts. *Shruti* texts are considered to be 'not of human origin', for they are believed to have been 'revealed' by the divine Brahma, the Creator, to certain inspired wise men of old. These wise men 'heard' the scriptures, and this is why the first Hindu scriptures are referred to as *shruti* (heard) texts.

? Writing was not used for religious purposes in India until the third century BCE. Why do you think this was so?

THE VEDAS

The Vedas are the oldest of the Hindu scriptures and were completed before the fifth century BCE. They are composed of four books, or collections of hymns – Rig-Veda, Yajur-Veda, Sama-Veda and Atharva-Veda. Within each of these four Vedas are four types of composition – the Mantras, the Brahmanas, the Aranyakas and the Upanishads.

Plan of the Vedas

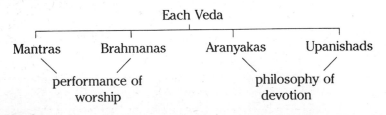

- The **Mantras**, or Psalms of Praise, constitute the main body of the Vedas and are the most ancient part.
- The **Brahmanas** are prose manuals of ritual and prayer for the guidance of priests. They were composed after the Mantras.
- The **Aranyakas** are the 'forest books' for hermits and saints, and were composed after the Brahmanas.
- The **Upanishads** are works on philosophy, composed after the 'forest books' towards the end of the period of Vedic literature.

The Contents of the Four Vedas

Rig-Veda

This is the most important and the oldest of the four Vedas. The text in its present form has survived from about 300 BCE. It is divided into ten books (called *mandalas*) and has 1028 hymns in praise of ancient deities. Some of these deities have been mentioned in Chapter 9.

Yajur-Veda

This is a priestly handbook to be used for the performance of sacrifices. The present text is in two collections, the older one is known as 'dark' (because of its obscure meanings), while the later one is the 'white' Yajur-Veda, because it brings 'order and light' to its meaning.

Sama-Veda

This Veda consists of melodies and chants. It indicates the 'tunes' for the sacred hymns to be sung at special sacrifices.

Atharva-Veda

This Veda contains the magical formulae of ancient India and much of it is devoted to spells, chants and charms. It has preserved to a great extent the pre-Aryan traditions.

Extracts from the Rig-Veda

As has already been mentioned, hymns in the Rig-Veda praise various deities controlling the forces of nature. Some selected verses from the Rig-Veda are set out below; the deities referred to in these hymns have particular relevance to modern Hinduism. Agni (Fire) is worshipped in *havan* (sacrifice); the Gayatri (Sun) hymn, as we saw in Chapter 3, is recited daily by many Hindus; Rudra, the chief of the storm deities, is now Shiva, the destroyer aspect of Brahman; and Vishnu, a deity of light in the Rig-Veda, is the preserver aspect of *Brahman* in modern Hinduism. Varuna has now receded into the background. The Purusha hymn provides religious justification for the *varna* divisions in Hindu society.

The extracts from the Rig-Veda below, as well as the extracts from the Upanishads and from the Bhagavad-Gita (see pages 72–3 and 79–80) have been translated and rendered into prose form by the author.

Agni

I praise Agni [God of Fire], who acts as the family priest, the officiating priest of the sacrifice, and the chief priest, as well as the giver of blessings. Agni is praised by ancient and modern wise men; may he summon the gods to be present at the sacrifice. May he who performs this sacrifice be blessed with success, wealth and brave sons. O God of Fire, the sacrificial offerings consumed by you must surely reach the gods.

From the Rig-Veda, I.1, verses 1–4.

Celebration of havan at the Shree Hindu temple, Bradford. A priest offers ghee and grain to Agni, the God of Fire.

Vishnu

Let me tell you about the powers of Vishnu, the God of Light [Aditya], who measured Earth and Heaven in three wide paces, which are three kinds of light in the form of Fire, Lightning and the Sun. [These three paces may also refer to the positions of the sun at rising, at noon and at setting.] For this heroic deed Vishnu is praised. He wanders at will like a fierce animal over mountains and the dwelling places of all creatures. May this hymn of praise rise up and give strength to Vishnu who dwells on the mountains. Like a striding bull he alone has measured out this wide world.

From the Rig-Veda, I.154, verses 1–3.

Rudra/Shiva

O Lord of the storm gods, may your grace come down to us [mortals]. Do not hide the sun from our sight. O Rudra, protect our horsemen from injury and may we have worthy children through your grace. You give us healing herbs which enable us to live a hundred years. O Rudra, remove all enmity, sorrow and disease from our lives. Your glory is unbounded, your strength unmatched among all living creatures, O Rudra, the wielder of the thunderbolt. Guide us safely to the far shore of existence where there is no sorrow. Protect us from injury and disease.

From the Rig-Veda, II.33, verses 1–3.

What kinds of people would you expect to offer worship to Rudra? Give reasons for your answer.

Gayatri

We concentrate our minds upon the most radiant light of the Sun God, who sustains the Earth, the Interspace and the Heavens. May the Sun God activate our thoughts.

From the Rig-Veda, III.62, verse 10.

Varuna

Sing a psalm of high praise in gratitude to Varuna, the Lord of the Waters, the mighty ruler [of the world]. He has spread out this earth in front of the sun as if it were the skin of a slain victim. He has placed air around the earth and in the trees of the forest; he has put milk in cattle and tireless speed in horses. He has endowed us with thoughts in our hearts; he has put power in the waters, placed the sun in Heaven and sowed the Soma plant on the mountains.

From the Rig-Veda, V.85, verses 1–2.

The Sacrifice of Primal Man – the Purusha Sukta

The Primal Man [Purusha] had a thousand heads, eyes and feet. [A 'thousand' here signifies a very large (infinite) number.] He filled the earth completely; indeed his body was larger than this world. The Primal Man fills this universe and represents the past and the future. He is eternal, and outgrows the universe by consuming sacrificial food. The visible world is only a quarter of his greatness; the remaining three-quarters is hidden in the immortal Heaven. From the performance of the complete sacrifice of Purusha came fourth the first three Vedas and the metres of the Vedas. From it also arose horses and other creatures with teeth in either jaw, like cattle, sheep and goats. When they split up Primal Man, into how many parts was He divided? What represented his mouth, arms, thighs and feet? The Brahmin was his mouth, the Kshatriya his arms, the Vaishya his thighs and the Shudra were born from his feet. [A priest uses his mouth for reciting and teaching scriptures, a soldier needs the strength in his arms to defend a country from its enemies, a merchant or a farmer uses his thighs for transporting goods for commerce or for working in a field, while an artisan provides services to three upper *varnas* just as the feet serve the body.]

From the Rig-Veda, X.90, verses 1–3 and 9–12.

What does the Vedic hymn called the 'Sacrifice of Primal Man' tell us about the caste system? Look at verse 12 ('The Brahmin was his mouth, the Kshatriya his arms, the Vaishya his thighs and the Shudra were born from his feet.') and explain who these four groups are and what the verse means.

THE UPANISHADS

These texts contain the mystical ideas of ancient Hindu philosophy. They are so named (*Upa-ni-shada* = sitting near) because they were originally tutorials given to select pupils who sat near their teacher to hear the sacred teaching. They have survived in their present form since about 200 BCE. Because they were composed at the end (*anta*) of the Vedic period, they form the basis of Vedanta philosophy.

The Content of the Upanishads

The Upanishads contain some of the most important ideas and topics of the Hindu religion:

- The individual soul (*atman*) and the universal soul (*Brahman*) are the same.

- *Brahman* is eternal, limitless and without form.
- The visible world is an illusion (*maya*).
- The total effect of actions (*karma*) decides the next existence of the soul.
- The soul exists through a cycle of successive births and deaths (*samsara*).
- The soul is capable of breaking the cycle of successive lives and deaths and achieving liberation (*moksha*).
- There is a one-ness of things throughout the created universe.
- The individual soul (*atman*) is never born and never dies.

The Upanishads also deal with: the nature of the soul; the relationship between the body, mind and senses; the various means of liberation; worship and meditation; and duties of a student.

Extracts from the Upanishads

These short extracts explain such philosophical ideas as:
- *atman* and *Brahman* are identical;
- *atman* is rehoused in a new body when the old one dies;
- *atman* gains liberation through selfless action;
- *Brahman* occupies the whole universe, although it cannot be perceived by human eye.

The stories of the fig seed and salt dissolved in water are told; and the relationship of *atman* to body, mind and intellect (the chariot story) is described. One extract offers advice to students.

Atman, karma *and* moksha

As a caterpillar crawls on a blade of grass and, when it reaches its tip, prepares to climb another blade, so does *atman* leave one body and, overcoming ignorance, prepare for its next lives, until it reaches *Brahman*. *Atman* is indeed *Brahman*, which consists of understanding, mind, senses, elements, desire, light, darkness, right and wrong. What a man becomes [in his next life] depends upon his *karma*. By good actions he attains merit, by bad actions he becomes evil. The *karma* of a man ruled by desire attaches to his *atman*, so that he is forced to suffer rebirth and return to the world of men. When all attachment arising from desires is destroyed, man's mortality ends, and only then does *atman* reach *Brahman* [i.e. attain liberation (*moksha*)].

From the Brihad-aranyaka Upanishad, IV.4, verses 3, 5 and 7.

? What do you think are the main differences between the man of desire and the man without desire? What awaits each of them at death? What is the purpose of returning to the world of men?

Advice to a student

Be truthful; follow your *dharma* [personal code of conduct]; never neglect your study of the scriptures; after you have completed your course and paid a fee to your teacher, marry and continue your family line by having sons; follow a righteous path; earn and spend money wisely; do not neglect your duties to gods and ancestors; honour your parents, teacher and guest; let your conduct be blameless and follow the example of your elders only in their righteous actions.

From the Taittiriya Upanishad, verse 11.

Selfless action

This whole universe is pervaded by Ishwara, the Lord. Be satisfied with whatever is your lot and do not desire things that belong to others. By performing sacrifices and other rituals and carrying out duties according to one's *dharma* [i.e. duties of one's *varna*, stage in life, caste], one should live for a hundred years. It is not possible to give up all action, but when actions are done as a duty, the burden of *karma* does not attach to the individual spirit.

From the Isha (Ishavasya) Upanishad, verses 1 and 2.

Self-control and moksha

Atman rides in a chariot which represents the body occupied by *atman*. Intellect is the driver of the chariot, the senses are the horses and the mind acts as reins. The senses range over various objects of desire in the same way as real horses cover a piece of ground. *Atman's* existence becomes successful [reduces the burden of *karma*] when mind controls the senses. He who does not know how to discipline the mind and control the senses, cannot control the chariot. He who lacks self-control does not escape the cycle of birth, death and rebirth, but he who has understanding breaks the cycle of *samsara* and attains liberation [*moksha*].

From the Katha Upanishad, III, verses 3–5 and 7–8.

One-ness of Brahman, atman *and all creation*

'O Svetaketu, bring me one of those figs over there,' said the father. The son obeyed his father and, having brought a fig, cut it open, as his father asked. He looked inside and told his father that he could see tiny fig seeds. 'Now, Svetaketu,' said his father, 'cut up a tiny seed and tell me what you see.' Svetaketu did as he was told and closely examined the cut-up seed, but he could not see anything. His father said: 'My son, you are not able to perceive the very essence from which this sacred fig tree grows. That essence is Reality. This whole universe has sprung from it. That essence is *atman* and you, Svetaketu, are also that essence.'

From the Chhandogya Upanishad, VI.12, verses 1–3.

Unity of Brahman, atman *and all creation*

Svetaketu's father gave him some salt, asked him to put it in water and keep the beaker in a safe place. The next morning his father asked Svetaketu to bring the beaker and take out the salt, but the task was impossible since the salt was completely dissolved. Svetaketu's father then asked his son to take sips from opposite sides of the beaker and describe the taste. 'It tastes of salt from both sides,' said Svetaketu. 'My son,' said his father, 'though you do not perceive it, the salt is there. Similarly you do not perceive that finest essence, the Universal Soul, yet it is here. That is Reality. That is *atman*, and you are also that essence.'

From the Chhandogya Upanishad, VI.13, verses 1–3.

?

1 According to these passages from the Upanishads, how should someone behave towards (a) the family; (b) other people; and (c) him- or herself?

2 Discuss the views of *Brahman* (God) given in the passages from the Upanishads. How do these views differ from those of the Vedic passages?

3 What seems to be the relationship between the individual soul (*atman*) and God (*Brahman*) in these selections of the Upanishads?

4 Act out the stories of the fig and the salt. Why do you think the teachers of the Upanishads used such methods?

The following table shows the four Vedas, the main Brahmanas and the most important Upanishads.

Vedas	Brahmanas	Upanishads
Rig-Veda	1 Aitareya 2 Kaushitaki	1 Aitareya 2 Kaushitaki
Sama-Veda	1 Chhandogya 2 Jaiminiya	1 Chhandogya 2 Kena
White Yajur-Veda	1 Shatapatha	1 Brihad-aranyaka 2 Isha
Black Yajur-Veda	1 Taittiriya	3 Taittiriya 4 Shvetashvatara 5 Maitrayani (Maitri) 6 Katha
Atharva-Veda		1 Mundaka 2 Mandukya 3 Prashna

RELEVANCE IN MODERN HINDUISM

The religious rituals and prayers used in daily worship and in *havan* (offerings made to the sacred fire) are based on the *shruti* texts. In addition, much of the basis of Hindu belief in reincarnation and in the relationship of the individual soul (*atman*) to God is to be found in the teachings of the Upanishads. All these aspects of the *shruti* texts are very much part of the 'living faith', and later scriptures are founded on the ideas first set out in the Vedas. For the educated Hindu of today, the scriptures include the Vedas, the 13 most important Upanishads and the Bhagavad-Gita (see Chapter 11).

Chapter 11

The Great Epics

SMRITI TEXTS

The great Hindu epics, the Mahabharata and the Ramayana, belong to what is known as *smriti* literature. *Smriti* texts include religious, moral and educational writings based on 'remembered' tradition. They were composed from the fifth century BCE onwards. The teaching of the *smriti* (that which is remembered) literature is valid for all devout Hindus as long as it does not contradict the *shruti* texts, which, as the direct revelation of God, remain supreme authority. *Smriti* literature is itemised below:

Smriti Literature

- **The Vedanga** This name is given to six texts composed after the Veda, but essential to Vedic study. They deal with ritual performance, law, astronomy, phonetics, grammar and literature.
- Texts on Hindu philosophy.
- Legendary texts, particularly the two Great Epics, the **Mahabharata** and the **Ramayana**.
- **The Puranas** These are old legends and myths retold for popular use.
- Subsidiary Vedas, including texts on medicine, music, archery, the science of wealth, architecture, and various arts and crafts.
- Texts of the worshippers of Shakti, the female energy in creation, usually identified as Parvati, wife of Shiva.
- The texts of various Hindu sects worshipping Vishnu, Shiva or the goddess Parvati (Shakti).

THE MAHA-BHARATA

This great Indian epic is based on an old legend. The earliest version is supposed to have been composed by Vyasa, a member of the royal Kuru family, which plays such a large part in the story. The present version appears to be the work of many authors, probably expanding between the fourth century BCE and the fourth century CE. It has 100 000 verses in 18 books (*parvas*), and around the central narrative many stories with a moral message are woven.

The Vedic Aryans were gradually extending their rule between the eighth and fourth centuries BCE; great social and political changes were taking place, and the concept of *dharma* (moral duty) had to be spread widely to bring order into the newly forming society. This was done through the Epics, which were recited at public ceremonies such as sacrifices. Writers deliberately included family and regional customs, and a variety of human types, in the stories. The establishment of *varna-ashrama-dharma*, and an emphasis on duty and truth, were the aims of the various authors of the Mahabharata.

The Central Story of the Mahabharata

The Mahabharata is essentially a story of a battle between good forces (the Pandavas) and evil ones (the Kauravas). It deals with the war between the Kuru princes and their cousins, the five sons of King Pandu. The conflict arose because the right to the throne was in dispute. The father of the Kuru princes was the eldest brother, but he was blind, and so his younger brother, Pandu, became king. When Pandu died, the blind elder brother assumed power at the capital, Hastinapur. Dharmaraj, the eldest son of Pandu, with his four brothers, Arjuna among them, and their mother, came to live at the capital.

All the princes were educated by two Brahmins, Drona and Kripa, in the use of weapons. One of Drona's sons and Karna, the son of a charioteer, were taught alongside the princes. The sons of Pandu soon became skilled in the use of clubs, swords and the bow and arrow. Although the Kuru princes and their friend Karna were also clever in handling arms, the Pandu princes, and particularly Arjuna, excelled them all in every respect. The Kuru princes were extremely jealous.

While the princes were still completing their education, the blind king appointed the eldest son of Pandu as heir to the throne. The Kuru princes resented this action and planned to kill their cousins in a fire. The Pandu princes escaped and went to live in disguise far away from the capital. During this time, Arjuna won an archery contest, for which the prize was the Princess Draupadi. Following the ancient custom of their family, Draupadi became wife to all five Pandu princes.

The Kuru princes were alarmed to discover that their cousins were still alive, and made further plans to destroy them. The blind king, in the meantime, had divided the kingdom, and the Pandu princes ruled their half from a new capital. Dharmaraj, the eldest son of Pandu, ruled wisely and the brothers prospered. This increased the jealousy of their cousins, who challenged the eldest Pandu prince to a gambling match.

The Kuru princes were greatly helped at this time by their maternal uncle, who played the game on their behalf using loaded dice and won every throw. Dharmaraj staked and lost his cattle, his city, his land, his whole kingdom; he even lost his four brothers. Finally he staked himself, and lost. Then the dice rolled one more time and he lost his wife, Draupadi. After this first game, all property was restored to the Pandu princes. Then there was a second game – and this time the loser was to be banished to a forest for 12 years and spend a thirteenth year without being recognised.

Dharmaraj lost the second game also; and so the Pandu princes and their wife, Draupadi, were banished for 13 years. (Many stories unconnected with the main tale are included in the Mahabharata and occur during the period of banishment.) Then, after the 13 years, the Pandu princes returned and demanded their rightful kingdom. Their Kuru cousins refused their claim, so both parties prepared for war. The fighting lasted for 18 days. The Kuru princes and their huge army were totally destroyed. The eldest son of Pandu ruled for many years, then gave up his kingship, and the brothers, accompanied by their wife, Draupadi, finally ascended to Heaven.

The Harivamsha

The supplement to the Mahabharata, called the Harivamsha, has over 16 000 verses and contains, among other subjects, an account of Krishna's birth and childhood adventures. Krishna, king of a neighbouring country, was Arjuna's brother-in-law, and so determined to help the Pandu princes in their war with the Kuru princes by becoming Arjuna's charioteer. Later Krishna was recognised as an incarnation of the god Vishnu.

1   Write a short speech from one of the Pandu princes giving your reasons for claiming back your kingdom.
2   What lessons might a Hindu grandmother expect children to learn when she tells them the story of the Mahabharata?

THE BHAGAVAD-GITA

The Bhagavad-Gita (Song of the Lord) is a philosophical text of 700 verses, divided into 18 chapters, and occurs in the sixth book of the Mahabharata. It was composed later than the Upanishads and is influenced by several schools of philosophy. Scholars believe that it reached its present form in about 300 CE, but it did not achieve popularity until the ninth century CE when the philosopher Shankara wrote a commentary on it. Today it is one of the most popular religious texts.

The Story of the Bhagavad-Gita

On the eve of the great Bharata war, Arjuna, the third son of Pandu, viewed the vast army of the Kuru princes. Seeing all his kinsmen ready to fight him, he was filled with remorse at the thought of killing his relations to gain a kingdom. He put down his bow and turned to his charioteer, Krishna, for guidance. It is Krishna's advice, which is given as a dialogue, that forms the text of the Gita.

On the right, Krishna, as charioteer, counsels Arjuna before the Bharata war. His words are passed on in the Bhagavad-Gita. On the first finger of his left hand Krishna spins his symbol, the discus, while Arjuna blows a conch shell to alert his troops.

The Message of the Bhagavad-Gita

In the poem, Krishna instructs Arjuna on moral and religious values and on man's relation to God. His arguments are drawn from three of the main schools of Hindu philosophy – Samkhya, Yoga, Vedanta – and the teachings of the Upanishads. The main themes stressed in the Gita are as follows:

- Everyone has a moral duty to work without expecting any return and to uphold *varna-ashrama-dharma*. So strongly does the Gita urge this doctrine of moral action that it goes so far as to say:

  > One's own *varna* duty, even badly performed, is better than another's *varna* duty, even if well executed.

- *Bhakti* (devotion to a personal god) is emphasised by Krishna. His teachings on the development and expression of this relationship of the worshipper to his god has had a lasting influence on the religious perceptions of Hindus through the centuries. (See the extracts from Chapters 12 and 18 of the Gita on page 80).

- The soul or *atman* is indestructible; after each existence it is reborn into a new body, which is determined by its actions in its previous life. One should not grieve over death, which is unavoidable, but should continue to perform one's social and moral duty to the best of one's ability. (See the extract from Chapter 2 of the Gita on page 79).

- The Supreme Spirit, *Brahman*, is eternal, and everything in the universe is a part of it. *Brahman* can be understood as all that is best in creation. Krishna lists the finest aspects of *Brahman*, and includes himself among them, thus showing Arjuna that he is divine and an incarnation of god Vishnu, the Preserver. (See the extract from Chapter 10 of the Gita below.) He makes this very clear in Chapter 4 of the Gita when he says:

> Whenever there is a rise of *adharma* [harmful conduct], and whenever faith declines, I appear in this world from age to age, to protect the good, to punish the wicked and to re-establish *dharma* [good order].

The Bhagavad-Gita contains a synthesis of different beliefs and states that the paths of knowledge, asceticism, action, yoga and devotion are all valid for achieving liberation (*moksha*) of the soul. For this reason, and in spite of adverse criticism by Hindu and non-Hindu scholars, the Gita is popular as a religious text among the large majority of Hindus.

Extracts from the Bhagavad-Gita

The verses from Chapter 2 of the Gita describe the nature of *atman* based on the ideas in the Upanishads. In the verses from Chapter 10 we see a reference to some of the Vedic deities such as Aditya (Vishnu), Rudra (Shiva), and Agni. Rama and Krishna are mentioned as incarnations of God (Vishnu). Verses from Chapters 12 and 18 are treated here in detail since they appear as 'specified texts' in a GCSE syllabus.

The nature of atman

Atman is not born and it never dies. It is eternal, everlasting and ancient. It is not destroyed when the body dies. If a man knows for certain that *atman* is constant and exists eternally, how can that man kill anyone or cause anyone's death? As a man throws away used and worn-out clothes and obtains new ones, so does *atman* leave worn-out bodies after death to enter new ones. Sharp weapons cannot cut *atman*, fire cannot burn it, the waters cannot make it wet and the wind cannot dry it up. Even if you think that *atman* is born and dies again and again, your grief is surely in vain, because everyone who is born must die and all who die are reborn; therefore do not grieve over this inevitable fact.

From Chapter 2, verses 20–3 and 26–7.

The Lord is everywhere

I am *atman* at the heart of all creatures; I am their origin, existence and decay. Among the deities of light I am Vishnu, among the stars the radiant Sun. Among the storm gods I am Marichi, and among the asterisms I am the moon. Among the *Rudras* I am Shankara [Shiva], among the demigods and demons I am Kubera, the Lord of Wealth. Among the *Vasus* I am Agni, and among the mountains I am Meru. Among the purifiers I am the

Wind, among the warriors I am Rama. Among the creatures living in water I am the crocodile, and among the rivers I am the holy Ganges. Among the Vrishni clan I am Vasudeva [Krishna], among the Pandavas I am Arjuna. Among the sages I am Vyasa and among the poets I am the poet Ushana.

From Chapter 10, verses 20–3, 31 and 37.

Bhakta

14 My devotee [*Bhakta*], who is ever content, constant in meditation, and exercises self-control, who has complete faith in Me, and has dedicated his mind and intellect to Me, is dear to Me.

15 He who does not disturb others and is not disturbed by the world, and who is free from joy, envy, fear and anxiety, is dear to Me.

16 He who expects nothing, is pure, skilful, unconcerned, untroubled, who has given up all selfish undertakings and is devoted to Me, is dear to Me.

17 He who is free from desires and sorrow, who neither rejoices nor hates, who has given up good and evil, and who is full of devotion, is dear to Me.

18–
19 He who treats friend and foe alike; accepts honour and insult with calmness; who treats heat and cold, pleasure and pain with a balanced mind; who has no attachment to worldly things; who treats censure and praise equally; who is silent, satisfied with little and has no home; and who has a steady mind full of devotion, that man is dear to Me.

20 The devotees who follow the immortal *dharma* just described, who have faith and have made Me their supreme goal, are exceedingly dear to Me.

From Chapter 12, verses 14–20.

Bhakti

65 Fix your mind on Me, show devotion for Me, perform sacrifice in My name, and offer Me *namaskar*. I truly promise, you are dear to Me.

66 Giving up all other paths approved by *dharma*, take refuge in Me. I will absolve you from all sins. Do not grieve.

67 This advice is never to be related by you to anyone who lacks penance or devotion, who does not render service, who does not wish to listen, or who abuses Me.

68 He who is supremely devoted to Me and imparts this most secret advice to my other devotees, will, without doubt, come to Me.

69 No other man will render Me better service than this; no other man on earth shall be dearer to me than he.

70 He who will study this sacred dialogue of ours will indeed worship Me through the path of knowledge; of this I am convinced.

71 The man full of faith and free from malice who hears this [dialogue] will be liberated, and shall attain the happy worlds reached by the righteous.

72 O Arjuna, have you concentrated fully on this advice? Is the delusion of your ignorance now destroyed?

Then Arjuna replied:

73 My confusion has been dispelled, I have again realised my responsibility through your Grace, O Krishna. My mind is firm, my doubts are gone. I will act according to your advice.

From Chapter 18, verses 65–73.

?

1 Describe the kind of person that Krishna wants his followers to be.

2 With a friend write a short play in which one of you, Arjuna, puts forward reasons for not fighting and the other, Krishna, argues why it is necessary to fight the Kurus.

THE RAMAYANA

This Epic developed from a popular folk ballad, and existed in a number of versions before reaching its final form. It occurs as a Buddhist tale, and later versions show signs of this Buddhist influence. The final version, relating the story of Prince Rama, is said to have been composed by Valmiki who, according to tradition, had lived as a robber in his youth. On the advice of a learned man, Valmiki gave up his old ways, took to study, and lived in a hermitage where he is supposed to have met the hero of his future poem and to have learned from him about his adventurous life.

Valmiki composed the story in simple verse. The incidents in the Ramayana took place before those in the Mahabharata, though the latter was composed first. In its present version the Ramayana contains 24 000 verses arranged into seven books. Scholars estimate that the Epic reached its final form between the second century BCE and the second century CE, but the seventh book, in which Rama is represented as an incarnation of Vishnu, was added later.

The Story of the Ramayana

King Dasharatha ruled over the country of Kosala from his capital, Ayodhya. He had three wives and four sons. Rama, the eldest son, was born to the senior queen, the middle queen gave birth to Lakshman and Shatrughna, while the son of the youngest queen, whom the king loved best, was Bharata. The four princes were educated in kingly duties and archery, along with other subjects. They grew up to be strong and handsome, and Rama and Lakshman became expert archers.

The archery contest

In their late teens, Rama and Lakshman were sent to protect the hermitage of a wise man from the attacks of demons, a task which the brothers did successfully. The wise man took them to the court of King Janaka in the kingdom of Mithila. There Rama won an archery contest by bending a large bow which many assembled kings and princes, among them Ravana, the powerful King of Lanka, had failed to do. King Janaka announced that Rama, the winner of the contest, would marry Sita, his daughter. The marriage was soon celebrated, and was attended by Rama's parents and the family priests. Rama's brothers married Sita's cousins, which pleased both the royal families.

Rama's banishment

When the family returned to Ayodhya, Dasharatha planned to make Rama heir to the throne. The youngest queen did not approve and demanded the fulfilment of two promises which Dasharatha had made when she had helped him win a battle. The king was duty bound to keep his word. The youngest queen demanded that her son, Bharata, be made heir-apparent and that Rama be banished from the kingdom for 14 years. Rama accepted his father's decision and, as an obedient son, he set out to live in the forest. His brother Lakshman, and his devoted wife Sita, also went into exile. Dasharatha soon died through grief, and Bharata ruled the kingdom in Rama's name.

Sita kidnapped

The three exiles stayed in the Dandaka forest for some years. One day, while Rama and Lakshman were out trying to catch a spotted deer to which Sita had taken a fancy, Sita herself was kidnapped by Ravana, who had come to their cottage as a holy man begging alms. The deer which had lured the brothers away from their cottage was a demon in disguise, helping Ravana, the King of Lanka. When Rama and his brother returned to the cottage, they discovered the plot and were filled with grief at the loss of Sita.

Hanuman finds Sita

They searched for Sita for many days, and in their wanderings came to a southern kingdom whose ruler, Sugriva, had been deposed by his brother. Rama promised to help Sugriva regain his throne and, in return, Sugriva sent his monkey general, Hanuman, to look for Sita. Hanuman searched for many days and finally he came to the island kingdom of Lanka, where he discovered Sita held a prisoner in the palace garden and guarded by fierce female demons.

Marble images of Hanuman, Lakshman, Rama and Sita, prepared for worship, in a north London temple.

Preparations for Sita's rescue

Rama and Sugriva collected a large army, crossed the ocean to Lanka and attacked Ravana's army. In one of the battles Lakshman was injured, but was revived by physicians using medicinal herbs which Hanuman had obtained. In the final battle Rama killed Ravana, rescued Sita and, after appointing Ravana's youngest brother to the throne of Lanka, returned to Ayodhya with Sita, Lakshman and the faithful Hanuman.

Rama's coronation

The people of the capital were happy to see Rama and Sita and celebrated their return with festivities. Rama was soon crowned, and the new king ruled over the kingdom with justice. Rama's spies informed him that his subjects doubted Sita's purity, since she had been a captive for many years. Sita assured Rama that she loved only him and that she was faithful to him.

Sita abandoned

Rama placed his kingly duties above his duties as a husband and, to please his subjects, he abandoned Sita, who was expecting their baby, near the hermitage of Valmiki. The old sage took care of her and, in due course, Sita gave birth to twins, Lawa and Kusha. Valmiki narrated this entire story to Sita's sons.

Sita found and lost again

Some years later, when Rama was performing a sacrifice, Valmiki brought Sita and the twins to the capital. Rama was overjoyed to see them. Sita once more protested her innocence and said that the earth would swallow her if she were pure. The earth immediately divided and Sita disappeared for ever. After some years Rama handed over the kingdom to his sons and gave up his earthly life.

The Moral Lessons of the Ramayana

The worship of Rama is very widespread throughout the Hindu world. Rama is the ideal of an obedient son, a devoted husband, a dutiful king, an affectionate brother, a brave warrior and a magnanimous conqueror. He held kingly duty above personal happiness; but his abandonment of his faithful wife, Sita, is a blemish in the story. Other characters are also presented as ideals of Aryan virtues – Sita, the faithful wife; Lakshman, the affectionate brother; and Hanuman, the devoted servant. Taken as a whole, the tale shows the constant struggle between good and evil forces in the world.

1   The story of the Ramayana is often told in India with the use of shadow puppets from behind a curtain. Produce such a play for the class, or perhaps for an assembly. You will need to divide the story into a number of scenes and to provide an introduction as well as the dialogue.

2   Write an epic poem, *The Ramayana*, based on the story. If possible, paint a series of pictures to illustrate it.

3   How does the Ramayana show the triumph of good over evil? How might someone use it to encourage a Hindu friend who is finding life difficult?

RELEVANCE OF THE EPICS IN MODERN HINDUISM

The Hindi version of the Ramayana by Tulsidas, as well as the recent musical Marathi version, *Geeta-Ramayana*, and the latest presentation of the Epic in 56 episodes on Indian television, continue to captivate millions of Hindus today, just as the original Sanskrit poem did in earlier centuries. So great a reverence do Hindus still have for the Ramayana, indeed, that rooms will be cleaned and television sets garlanded before a family sits down to watch the next episode of the television serial.

To a large extent the Great Epics and the Bhagavad-Gita have been instrumental in the spread of Hindu culture and in the establishment of *varna-ashrama-dharma* in India.

<table>
<tr><td>

Chapter

12

</td><td>

Later Scriptures

</td></tr>
</table>

THE LAW BOOKS (*DHARMA-SHASTRAS*)

The Hindu word for a law book is *dharma-shastra*, which literally means the science of a code of conduct. These law books, written between 300 BCE and 600 CE, give rules of conduct for various classes (*varna*) of people at different stages of life (*ashrama*). They are *smriti* texts (see Chapter 11), since they preserve ancient traditions and practices. There are many law books, but the most important ones are those compiled by Manu, Yajnavalkya, Parashara and Narada.

Manu-Smriti (the Code of Manu)

The law book of Manu firmly upholds *varna-ashrama-dharma* and the four aims of human life. It deals with religious practice, law, custom and politics, and stresses that the *varna* divisions are based on natural talents and on the ability to do certain types of jobs. Manu states that women should be honoured and made happy in their husbands' families, and that a woman need not marry if a suitable husband is not found for her. The Code of Manu gives divine sanction to the caste system. It is revered by the Brahmins, but is rejected by other castes.

The present text, compiled in about 300 CE, has over 2600 verses arranged in 12 books, and deals with about 30 different topics concerning the Hindu way of life.

Page from an ancient Sanskrit manuscript, showing the decorative border and elaborate, clear script.

The present Hindu law, which applies only to Hindus, and is based on these ancient *dharma-shastras*, deals with family property, inheritance, marriage, adoption and guardianship. Since the 1955 legislation by the Indian Parliament, divorce is allowed to Hindus, as it is to the other religious groups in India. All other legal matters are governed by Indian secular law, which applies to all Indian citizens.

OLD MYTHS AND LEGENDS (THE PURANAS)

These texts belong to the religious literature of the later form of Indian religion, which we recognise today as 'Hinduism'. They deal with the worship of later deities, particularly Brahma, Vishnu and Shiva. The Puranas are closely connected with the two Great Epics and are used mainly by temple priests. They were composed between the sixth and sixteenth centuries CE. There are many minor works, but, traditionally, there are 18 important Puranas:

The Important Puranas

those glorifying Brahma	*those glorifying Vishnu*	*those glorifying Shiva*
• Brahma	• Vishnu	• Matsya
• Brahmanda	• Naradiya	• Kurma
• Brahma-vaivarta	• Padma	• Linga
• Markandeya	• Bhagavata	• Vayu
• Bhavishya	• Garuda	• Skanda
• Vamana	• Varaha	• Agni

The Bhagavata Purana

This is the most widely read and well-known text for the worshippers of Vishnu. The numerous manuscripts and printed editions, and the many commentaries and translations of the text, are proof of the wide influence of this Purana throughout the Hindu world. It probably originates from the tenth century CE. The text is divided into 12 books and has about 18 000 verses. The legends praise and glorify Vishnu, and his *avatars* (incarnations) are described in detail. The tenth book, which supplies a detailed biography of Krishna, is the most frequently read; the eleventh book tells of the total destruction of the clan of the Yadavas and of the death of Krishna.

RELIGIOUS LITERATURE IN CONTEXT

The Vedas, the Upanishads, the Vedanta-Sutras (which form the basis of Vedic philosophy), the Bhagavad-Gita, and the texts and commentaries connected with the six systems of Hindu philosophy, represent the theory of *Sanatana-dharma*; while the Law Books, the Epics and the Puranas reflect the practical aspects of popular

Hinduism. The Puranas are based on old myths and legends, retold for popular consumption; they are often recited in temples at festival times, so that even the illiterate can learn the myths and legends of ancient Hinduism.

1 What religious purpose do the Puranas have for Hindus?
2 List the ways in which people in a Hindu village are likely to be educated in their religion. Which methods do you think are likely to be most effective?
3 Many Hindus learn about their religion from stories told to them when they are children. Why do Hindus consider this a valuable method?

Chapter 13

Development of the Faith

Most scholars believe that the Vedic literature was completed by the eighth century BCE, and that by the end of the seventh century BCE, north Indian society was organised into three main categories. This newly forming society was gradually moving eastwards from the Indus valley and the Punjab into the vast Indian plain watered by the rivers Jumna (Yamuna) and Ganges (Ganga).

The character of the new society was changing too; the Aryans were no longer nomads from central Asia; they had by now adapted religious ideas from the original civilisation and intermarried with the earlier inhabitants, and new settlements had sprung up. As a result, various skills were being developed to provide goods and services to the settlements.

VARNA DIVISIONS

The *varna* classification of ancient Hindu society has been described in Chapters 5 and 6. These divisions, namely Brahmin, Kshatriya, Vaishya and Shudra, were based on the Purusha hymn (*Purusha* means 'Cosmic Person' or 'Primal Man'), which occurs in the tenth book of the Rig-Veda (see Chapter 9). The Purusha hymn gives a divine sanction to the *varna* classification and suggests that different people have different talents and potentials which determine their natures. This was the basis on which the *varna* groups were formed.

Functions of the Four *Varnas*

The Brahmins were priests, concerned with the performance of rituals and sacrifices, and learning and teaching the scriptures. The Kshatriyas were warriors and rulers, who governed and defended the settlements against external enemies. The Vaishyas used their talents for commerce and agriculture. Gradually a fourth *varna*, called Shudras, was added to the earlier three-fold division. This new *varna* consisted of artisans who provided goods and services to the three earlier groups.

A modern Kshatriya: Private Kamal Ram, the youngest Indian VC of World War II. He is shown wearing his Victoria Cross with pride.

People outside the *Varna* Divisions

There were also a large number of families engaged in what were considered 'unclean' occupations, such as tanning leather and removing dead animals from the villages. These people belonged to the Panchama (fifth) group, and they were excluded from the *varna* classification. Because of the dirty and degrading nature of their work, they lived at one end of the village away from the people who did 'clean' jobs, as, indeed, they still do in many Indian villages.

Visitors at a leather-worker's home. The woman in the centre of the picture carries a traditional sweeper's broom of twigs.

CASTE (*JATI*)

Gradually, different occupational groups (castes) developed within the *varna* divisions. The skills and trade secrets of each craft were jealously guarded within families, where sons learned the techniques of their fathers' occupations. This was the easiest method of passing knowledge on to the next generation, and led to the practice of boys following on in the occupations of their fathers.

This, however, had not always been the case. In the early period of Hindu society, it was possible for some people to change their occupations, and to move either up or down the *varna* divisions. According to the Code of Manu (compiled in the third century CE, but based on earlier texts such as the Purusha hymn), a Brahmin could take up Vaishya occupations, just as a Vaishya could take up Kshatriya occupations. But those doing 'unclean' jobs had no hope of improving their lot and were condemned to remain at the bottom of the social scale.

The Origins of Caste

With the passing of the centuries, various occupations, from the priests at the top to the leather-workers at the bottom of society, became exclusive, and because of the vested interests of each group in its own particular field, it became increasingly difficult for people to change from one occupation to another. All types of work became hereditary in nature and this, coupled with exclusiveness, gave rise to certain rules prohibiting interdining and intermarriage between the occupational groups, or castes. These castes were fitted into the four main *varna* divisions, so that a hierarchy based on occupation emerged.

The hierarchical ranking of individual castes within the *varna* system was not the same all over India, though the *varna* ranking itself was. For example, within the Shudra group, the washerman-caste might rank above the barbers in some places, but below them in others; yet they would all remain Shudras, and rank below Brahmins, Kshatriyas and Vaishyas. 'Caste' and '*varna*' are therefore not interchangeable terms or concepts.

Different Castes in the same *Varna*

A *varna* is a larger group and within it are many castes doing different types of jobs and following different family traditions and practices. The following two examples show how people of different castes within the same *varna* do things slightly differently because of their jobs and caste traditions.

Pandit Keshava

Pandit Keshava is a Brahmin living in a village, where he conducts various home-based rituals and *pujas* for certain families as a professional priest. He does not, however, do any funeral rituals. These are conducted by another priest, who, because he is associated with the pollution that death is thought to bring, has a lower ritual status.

Keshava worships Vishnu, Shiva and goddess Parvati at different festivals. He rises early, bathes and, after offering water to the rising sun, performs *puja* at the household shrine. He then conducts morning *pujas* at the houses of his four patrons. This lasts for over four hours, so he does not have his morning tea until 10 a.m. His wife and son also get up early, bathe and offer prayers at the family shrine. The boy attends the village primary school and, in the late afternoon, he learns *mantras* for various *pujas* from his father.

A village Brahmin priest wearing the sacred thread. He stands by an image of Nandi, the bull sacred to Shiva.

Keshava's family are strict vegetarians, teetotal and non-smokers. Keshava conducts rituals for the three upper *varnas* in the village and he is paid grain, vegetables and some cash in return. On the day of Krishna's birth festival, and on Mahashivaratri day, he observes a complete fast. His daily routine is strict; he eats only at the houses of fellow caste-members and never takes tea in a café when he visits the nearby market town.

Gopal

Gopal is also a Brahmin and teaches in the village school. He too rises early, bathes and performs a simple *puja* at the household shrine. His wife and two daughters rise early, bathe and, after offering *namaskar* to the family deities, have tea. The younger daughter attends primary school, while the elder teenage daughter helps her mother with housework. Sometimes Gopal's wife performs morning *puja*, and on those days Gopal takes tea before bathing. He gives private tuition to the son of a rich farmer on three mornings each week and saves the extra earnings for his elder daughter's marriage. Gopal's family celebrate only Shiva and Parvati festivals. Their caste tradition allows them to eat fish, except on festival days which are strictly vegetarian. Gopal's religious rituals are few, but he reads a short prayer to Shiva and recites the Gayatri hymn before going to his teaching job. Gopal has occasional meals at the houses of other Brahmin castes and, when he visits the market town, he does not hesitate to take tea in a café and smoke an occasional cigarette.

What difficulties would arise if Gopal suggested that his daughter marry into Keshava's family?

THE FIVE PRINCIPLES OF CASTE

The term 'caste' is derived from the Portuguese word *casta* (race, kind, breed) and is applied to thousands of occupational groups in Hindu society. The Indian term for caste is *jati*. The social manifestation of caste is seen in five ways:

Pollution

Members of the upper castes consider the low castes to be unclean. They believe that they can be polluted by these people in several ways – by being near them, by eating the same cooked food, or by using the same well. The 'untouchables' were therefore kept well away; the lowest ebb of their status was reached when the priests, the rulers and the merchants avoided their touch and even their shadows for fear of ritual pollution.

Commensality

Commensality means eating together or interdining. The general rule in Hindu society today is that members of the same caste eat together, and that only fellow caste-members are invited to a meal in the home after a home-based ritual. Higher castes are afraid of the ritual pollution that may arise from eating forbidden foods, such as meat, fish and, in some cases, onion and garlic. Difficulties arise, however, when different castes in a village are all invited to a wedding feast. On such occasions, each caste sits in a separate row, thus creating an area of privacy for itself and enabling all to eat at the same time, but 'not together'. The cooks usually have to be Brahmins, since food cooked by Brahmins does not pollute other castes.

Endogamy

This means that, generally, a marriage partner for a young man or woman is chosen from the same caste, although inter-caste marriages are now legal. Nowadays it is possible for young people from different castes to make a personal choice to marry, and they will probably get their parents' approval if the two families are modern in outlook and are of the same economic class. When marriages are arranged by parents, the choice of a boy or a girl from the same caste assures that the two families will have equal status in social, financial and cultural matters.

Hereditary Occupation

For many centuries, as we have seen, sons followed on in their fathers' occupations. In modern India, greater educational opportunity has enabled young people to train in different fields and to apply for jobs which are open to all, regardless of caste. Young people from professional homes are still more likely to go on to higher education and to follow their fathers' professions, because study is a tradition in such families and they can afford higher education. But many people from lower castes have managed to achieve high status jobs, with the result that hereditary occupation as an aspect of caste is no longer very important in modern India.

Economic Interdependence

Certain lower castes such as the village barber, the washerman, or the oilman used to perform services for the higher castes and were rewarded in kind. These 'service-castes' received a share of the grain from their farming patrons at harvest time. Some Brahmins acted as priests or teachers to Kshatriya or Vaishya castes on the same basis. Although 'payment in kind for services performed' is still practised in many villages, the cash wages that can be earned in factories diminish this economic interdependence in modern India.

1   Ritual pollution is a very important idea in Hinduism, as well as moral pollution. What do they mean? Discuss how Hindus believe they can be removed.

2   Imagine you are a Hindu parent. Explain to your son why it is important that he should marry a girl from the same caste as himself. (Remember to refer to each of the five principles of caste in giving your answer.)

3   What value might a barber or weaver say there was in the principle of hereditary occupation? Why might their sons disagree with them? Why might members of the water-carrying caste disagree even more strongly?

CASTE IN MODERN HINDU SOCIETY

From the beginning of this century, caste barriers have gradually been broken down in matters of interdining and social mixing, particularly in the large cities of India. When India became a secular republic in 1950, untouchability was abolished by law. Hindu temples were declared 'open' for all Hindus, and positive discrimination through legislation provided opportunities for education and jobs to the underprivileged sections of society. Caste and *varna* are still important in relation to marriage, whether in India or overseas where Hindus have settled, and only fellow caste- or *varna*-members are invited to take part in religious rituals and ceremonies celebrated in the home. Caste ties may be dormant until time of need, for instance during elections or when applying for jobs in modern industrial concerns, when they are readily activated.

1   Sometimes caste seems to matter very little today, except when it comes to marriage – most are arranged between families of the same caste. Why do you think this is?

2   Imagine you are a Brahmin. How would you defend the caste system and your position in it?
Now imagine that you are a member of the 'scheduled classes', often called 'untouchable' in the past. On what grounds might you (a) support the Brahmin; and (b) oppose the system?

Chapter 14

The Hindu Idea of God

The Hindu idea of God developed from the beginnings of the Rig-Veda in about 1200 BCE to the completion of the earliest Puranas at the end of the sixth century CE. The early hymns of the Rig-Veda praise the spirits of the natural forces such as Fire, Thunder, Sky, Dawn, Water, Rain, Earth and the Sun. Although some deities such as Dawn and Earth are feminine, the majority of Vedic deities are male. The hymns praised individual deities, but the Vedic sages had formed the idea that the various deities were really different aspects of One Supreme Power. They called the Supreme Power 'Truth'. This concept is expressed in the line from the Rig-Veda, *Ekam sat vipra bahuda vadanti* ('Truth is One; wise men call it by different names'). This is how the underlying principle of unity was expressed in Vedic times.

HOW MANY GODS?

The Vedic Deities

There are 33 principal deities in the Vedas, divided into several categories:

* eight *Vasus*, the guardians of eight directions
* 11 *Rudras*, the storm deities
* 12 *Adityas*, the deities of light
* Indra, the Lord of Heaven
* Prajapati, the Lord of Creatures

Within these categories, these 33 deities remain distinct, each having a personal responsibility. For example, some of the 12 *Adityas* are: Varuna (one who surrounds and binds), Daksha (the skilful), Mitra (the friend), Bhaga (the giver), Aryaman (the destroyer), Savita (the enlightener) and Vishnu (the all-pervader). For this reason, they are considered in modern Hinduism to be of 33 different 'kinds' or 'types', a translation of the Sanskrit word *koti*. This word has led to confusion, since it also means a crore (1 crore = 10 million). This difference in meaning has led to the saying that 'Hindus worship 330 million gods', whereas in fact this should read 'Hindus worship 33 deities of distinctive types' which, of course, actually represent the various aspects of One Supreme Reality.

The Deities of Modern Hinduism

The Upanishads and the Vedanta system of philosophy gave a new name to the 'Truth' of the Vedas. In the Upanishads, the Supreme

Spirit is called *Brahman*, and is without quality (*guna*) or form (*akara*), and can be male or female. *Brahman* controls the created world through its three major aspects, whose origins are in the Vedas. The Vedic god Prajapati is called Brahma in Hinduism; one of the *Adityas* becomes a prominent aspect of *Brahman* and is identified as Vishnu; Rudra of the Vedas is combined with the male deity of the non-Aryan Indus people to become Shiva. Thus the *Trimurti*, that is Brahma, Vishnu and Shiva, begin to become prominent deities in the post-Upanishad period. Agni (Fire) and Savita (Sun) continue to be worshipped in Hinduism, but other Vedic deities like Indra, Varuna, Soma and Parjanya have receded into the background. The names of the deities have changed, but the principle of unity contained in the Vedas continues in modern Hinduism.

As we saw in Chapter 1, Brahma creates the world, Vishnu preserves and protects it, and Shiva destroys a part of it at a time so that Brahma can continue his work of creation. The female counterparts of the male deities in the *Trimurti* are Saraswati, Laxmi and Parvati respectively.

AVATAR (INCARNATION) AND IMAGE WORSHIP

The Bhagavad-Gita in the Mahabharata was probably responsible for the popularisation of earlier ideas of *avatar* (incarnation) of a saviour God and the use of images as symbols of deities to be used in worship. Some of the Puranas mention *avatars* of Shiva, but the *avatar* concept is usually associated with Vishnu, the preserver of the world. In the fourth chapter of the Gita, Lord Krishna says:

> To protect the good, to punish the wicked and to establish *dharma*, I reincarnate myself from age to age.

Vishnu is believed to have appeared on earth in ten *avatars* to protect humanity. His traditional incarnations are:

- Fish
- Tortoise
- Boar
- Man-Lion
- Dwarf
- Parashurama with an axe
- Rama (the hero of the Ramayana)
- Krishna
- Buddha
- Kalki, the rider on a white horse

This last incarnation, still to come, is believed to appear when the end of the world approaches.

In the twelfth chapter of the Gita, Arjuna says:

> Lord, which of your devotees are better versed in devotion, those who worship your image or those who worship you as the formless spirit?

Lord Krishna replies that He prefers those who offer worship to an image, since the other method is difficult for ordinary mortals:

> But those of my devotees who worship Me as formless *Brahman* also come to Me.

An ancient stone sculpture showing Vishnu seated on the serpent, Shesha. The small image to the left is the divine eagle, Garuda, while on the right is Hanuman.

Some Important Hindu Deities

The conversation between Arjuna and Lord Krishna, quoted above, refers to image worship, which was becoming more widespread in the fourth century BCE. It is important to remember that images are an *aid* to worship and not *objects* of worship in Hinduism. The images of different gods and goddesses have arisen from man's imagination. Hindus have full freedom to imagine *Brahman* represented in any form, male or female, human, animal or bird, or a combination of these. The images and the symbolism of some important deities in Hinduism are described below:

Brahma

Brahma has four faces, is seated on a lotus and holds a book, a rosary and a gourd. He is the creator aspect of *Brahman*.

Saraswati

The consort of Brahma, Saraswati is the Goddess of Learning and the Arts. She holds a book and a *veena* (a musical instrument), and her *vahana* (vehicle) is a peacock or a swan.

Vishnu

The preserver aspect of *Brahman*, Vishnu has four arms and he holds a conch shell, a discus, a lotus and a mace. His vehicle is the divine eagle, Garuda. Rama and Krishna are the most important *avatars* of Vishnu.

Laxmi

Laxmi is Vishnu's wife, and the Goddess of Good Fortune. She is depicted as a woman of beauty, modesty and gentleness, fully clothed, and standing in a lotus, rewarding the worshipper with gold.

Shiva

The destroyer aspect of *Brahman*, Shiva is worshipped as a deity of fertility and regeneration. He holds a trident, a rosary and a gourd. He has a serpent round his neck and the crescent moon in his coiled hair. He is also depicted as a great yogi and the Lord of the Beasts. His vehicle is Nandi, the bull.

Nataraj (Shiva)

Shiva is often represented as Nataraj, performing the dance of creation. The Dancing Shiva image shows: the river Ganga in his hair, a drum in his right hand for the rhythm of the dance of creation, a serpent (cobra), his right hand granting freedom from fear, his left foot raised signifying salvation, a crescent moon in his coiled hair, his left hand holding sacred fire (destruction and re-creation of the world), the circle of glory (the universe), and ignorance being trampled underfoot.

Nataraj (Shiva).

An image of Ganesha at the Shree Hindu temple, Bradford. He is shown garlanded and seated on a lotus, holding his emblems and attended by his vehicle, the mouse.

Parvati

Parvati is Shiva's wife and is worshipped as Shakti, the female energy in creation. In her mild and gentle appearance she is the Mother Goddess, but she is also worshipped in other appearances (see below). In different regions and communities she is worshipped as the local deity under such names as Amba-Mata, Amma, Santoshi-Mata – all of which mean 'mother'.

Durga

Durga is the warlike form of Parvati, riding a tiger and holding many weapons in her eight arms.

Kali

A grotesque image of Parvati, Kali is represented as a bloodthirsty deity demanding blood-sacrifices.

Ganesha (Ganapati)

Ganesha was created by Parvati, and is considered as a son by Parvati and Shiva. He has a large human body with four arms, and an elephant's head with only one short tusk. He holds a snare in one hand, and a goad and an axe in the other; with the third hand he offers sweetmeats to his devotees and he uses the fourth hand to bless the worshipper. Ganesha is the remover of obstacles and he is worshipped at the beginning of *pujas* as well as at the start of important undertakings. His vehicle is a mouse.

Subrahmanya

The second son of Shiva and Parvati, Subrahmanya is also called Kartikeya and is popularly worshipped in south India.

Hanuman

The monkey general of Rama, Hanuman is famous for his exploits in the Ramayana. He holds an Indian club and is the deity of physical culture. The Hanuman temple is a feature of many villages in western India.

'The presence of many deities proves that there is polytheism in the Hindu faith.' Do you agree?

HOW IMAGES ARE MADE

The materials used for making images are clay, red earth, plaster of Paris, white marble, wood, or black or gray stone.

Image-making is a family business going back several generations in the families concerned, and the artisans come from a wide cross-section of society. Marble images are carved in many villages around Jaipur in north India, and black or gray stone images are made in the south. Both types are used in temples. Clay images of various deities are made locally all over India and are used in the celebrations of seasonal festivals. Small images made from plaster of Paris and sandalwood are used in many household shrines, while large wooden images are used for the annual chariot processions at important temples.

No special religious rituals are undertaken by the image-makers, but during certain festive seasons, such as Ganesha, Navaratri and Diwali, when many images are made and sold, the image-makers avoid eating meat and fish. Images are worshipped as symbols of deities only after the 'consecration *puja*', when the spirit of God is believed to enter them.

Most Hindu temples in Britain, as well as Hindu homes, have examples of these images which are imported specially from India.

MAIN DIVISIONS OF HINDU WORSHIP

Hindus fall into three main categories of worshippers: those whose primary devotion is to Vishnu and his incarnations; those who worship Shiva as the principal deity; and those who worship Shakti, the female principle in creation, usually termed the Mother Goddess and identified with Parvati. The main deity worshipped depends on family tradition, but it is important to note that this does not imply exclusivity in Hindu worship. For example, the god Ganesha, the son of Parvati and Shiva, is worshipped by followers of Vishnu before they undertake any new enterprise as well as at the beginning of any *puja*. The various sects of Hinduism are placed within these three traditions.

?

1   Hindus enjoy great freedom in matters of belief. People in the same family might worship different gods. Which god or goddess might you choose if you were a Hindu? Why? Try to collect some pictures or even a statue and find out some of the stories (myths) about the god you have selected.

2   Hindus believe that God is one, though people call the One God by many names and worship the One God in many forms. Imagine you are a Hindu, and try to explain this idea to a friend who is of another religion or even of no religion.

3   Hindus are sometimes accused of worshipping idols. What is an 'idol'? How might a Hindu answer this charge?

4   Explain the help Hindus obtain from using images in worship.

5   Some Hindus would not use images, though they would recognise their value for other people. Imagine that your grandparents come to visit you and are surprised to find no pictures of the gods or their images in your home. How would you gently explain your views, taking care not to offend them? You might put it into the form of a play.

Chapter 15

Philosophical Concepts in Hinduism

This chapter attempts to explain some important but difficult concepts of Hindu philosophy. The soul and its relationship to the material world occupy the first half, while the second half deals with the soul's liberation from the cycle of successive births. It is important to note that the word '*karma*' is used here to mean 'the result of one's actions in a previous birth', while the same word carried a different meaning in Chapter 7.

THE SOUL AND ITS RELATION- SHIP TO THE MATERIAL WORLD

Atman

According to the Vedanta philosophy and the Bhagavad-Gita, *atman* is the divine and animating energy in every creature. It is indestructible and continues to exist after the body dies, when it is rehoused in a new body. Each *atman*, because of the result of its actions, goes through a series of lives until it achieves liberation from the cycle of successive rebirths.

Shankara, the great philosopher who lived in the ninth century CE, held that *atman* and *Brahman* were identical; Ramanuja, in the eleventh century CE, maintained that, although a part of *Brahman* and dependent upon it, *atman* does not fully merge with *Brahman* when it gains liberation; Madhava, in the thirteenth century CE, stated that *atman* and *Brahman* were quite separate.

Prakriti

Prakriti is the matter necessary for all creation, but in its primordial or original state before the forces of nature have been created from it. Purusha, the First Being, animates it, and so begins the process of creation. All material things come from and are of *prakriti*. *Prakriti* enables *atman* to go through successive lives.

Gunas

Every created object, including human beings, has three qualities built into its make-up and character. These qualities are called *gunas*; they are *sattva* (high, forces of light), *rajas* (middle, forces of desire) and *tamas* (low, forces of darkness and ignorance). The nature of each man, woman and child is influenced by the strongest *guna* in his or her constitution. The influence of *gunas* also affects human actions, which in turn trap *atman* in the cycle of successive lives.

Maya

Maya is described by Shankara in his commentary on the Vedanta-Sutras as an illusion. (*Sutras* are concise verses explaining a particular topic such as ritual, grammar, or Vedanta philosophy.) Since the material world is dependent upon perishable and changing matter for its existence, everything the eye sees is impermanent and an illusion, which is the result of *maya*.

THE SOUL'S PATH TO LIBERATION FROM REBIRTH

Dharma

We have already considered the nature of *dharma* in Chapter 5 in connection with *varna*, *ashrama* and the aims of life. *Dharma* is the individual's personal code of conduct; it is to be followed in all situations to effect correct practice. In Hinduism, practice takes priority over belief; each person is required to act according to personal *dharma* in carrying out *varna*, *ashrama*, *jati* and family duties, in the pursuit of wealth and in the enjoyment of the good things of life. *Dharma* is the main vehicle for *atman* in its journey towards liberation.

Karma

Karma is the total effect of an individual's good or bad actions. The burden of *karma* does not attach to *atman* if a person's actions are performed selflessly and always according to *dharma*. *Dharma* guides the individual *atman* towards final liberation from constant rebirth. The bodies which the individual *atman* occupies in successive lives are determined by its *karma* in a previous existence.

Samsara

The cycle of birth, death and rebirth is termed *samsara*. It is long but not endless, since every *atman* is capable of reaching its final goal, to be near or united with the Supreme Reality, thus achieving liberation from repeated births and deaths. *Karma* binds *atman* to *samsara*; when the burden of *karma* is lifted through righteous, dutiful living, *atman* is able to break the cycle of *samsara*.

Moksha

This is the final stage of existence, when *atman* is freed from *samsara*. This stage depends upon both *dharma* and *karma*. *Karma* means both the total effect of action and action itself. The snares of *karma* are increased as an individual progresses through the various stages of life and pursues wealth and enjoyment; nevertheless, transit through the *ashramas* is essential for human development. It is difficult for most individuals to ignore the material world, and the only way to free *atman* from the temptations of this world is to satisfy desires by earning money and enjoying the good things of life. Hinduism encourages everyone to achieve material success, but this should never become the only goal of one's life; the final aim is to enable *atman* to achieve *moksha*.

Hindus believe that beings who do not attain *moksha* return to another existence. The idea is based upon the scriptures, but are there any other arguments which a believer in *samsara* might use in trying to persuade a non-Hindu?

DIFFERENT PATHS OF LIBERATION

Chapter 7 described the five ways of expressing belief through daily life. Now we can see how four of these paths also lead to release from constant rebirth. These paths are recommended in the Bhagavad-Gita:

The Path of Knowledge

This path, under the guidance of a teacher, brings enlightenment and leads to *moksha*, but is difficult for most individuals.

The Path of Yoga

The path of yoga needs a teacher to guide an individual in exercises and meditation. After many years' study, *atman* can achieve *moksha* in this way.

The Path of *Bhakti*

The path of *bhakti* involves devotion to an *ishwara* or an *ishta-devata* (personal deity) and is open to all Hindus irrespective of their social or ritual status. Every action is to be offered to an *ishwara* as a sacrifice, until *atman* attains liberation.

The Path of *Karma*

The path of *karma* (actions) also leads the soul towards *moksha*. Every action throughout life must be performed according to

A woman devotee of Krishna offering worship to her ishwara, *or personal deity.*

dharma and without expecting any reward. Only then will the burden of *karma* not attach to *atman*. This does not mean that individuals have to go through life without receiving just and fair rewards for their labour. Selfless action means action performed as *dharmic* duty, not action with an ulterior motive. To do a job as a duty, according to *dharma*, is considered the easiest form of worship, and the path of *karma* the simplest way to lead *atman* to final liberation.

Atman achieves *moksha* when it is able to break the cycle of *samsara*; in this belief, the philosophers Shankara, Ramanuja and Madhava, whatever their differences, stand united.

1 How might a Hindu reply to someone who argued that the *karma* theory discouraged him or her from being concerned about his/her material welfare?
2 If you were a Hindu, how would you explain your present life on the basis of the theory of *karma*?

Chapter 16

Modern Movements and their Leaders

CONTACT WITH THE WEST

In 1498 CE, India began a new historical phase. Vasco da Gama, a Portuguese explorer, discovered a sea route to India by sailing round Africa and he landed at Calicut on the Malabar coast. After this, many European adventurers from France, Holland, Denmark, Portugal and Britain came to India for trade. All of them, except the Danes, set up trading establishments in ports such as Surat, Bombay, Goa, Vengurla, Madras, Pondicherry and Calcutta. The Portuguese and the British established their political sway over many areas.

These new invaders had a profound influence on India's social, political and religious life. Indians came into contact with Western seamanship, weapons of war, science, European (and particularly English) literature and European Christian missionaries. The British East India Company laid the foundations of British rule in India when Robert Clive won the battle of Plassey in 1757. By 1780, the Company's rule was firmly established in Bengal, and Indians were employed in large numbers as clerks, minor revenue officials and common soldiers. This kind of contact with very different and challenging cultural patterns gave rise to new ideas and intellectual perspectives in India, which resulted in the development of modern movements in Hinduism.

RAM MOHAN ROY (1772–1833)

Ram Mohan Roy was born into a Brahmin family at Bardwan, Bengal, and experienced the orthodox practice of Hinduism in his childhood and youth. He was sent to Patna, where he studied the Q'ran in the original and read the poetry of the Persian Sufi poets, which led him to form a dislike of image worship in Hinduism. He then went to Tibet to study Buddhism. After his travels he settled in Banaras in order to study the Hindu scriptures. He took a job with the British East India Company and, in 1809, was appointed a revenue official. In about 1800, he formed a religious reform society in Calcutta, and through contact with missionaries he studied the New Testament.

In 1811 he came into direct contact with the practice of suttee, when his brother's widow, in spite of her protests, was burned alive on her husband's funeral pyre. He campaigned for the abolition of the practice, which was eventually effected by Lord William Bentinck in 1829. In order to be free to do his work of social and religious reform, he retired from the Company's service in 1814. He published a book on Vedanta, but rejected the theory of reincarnation of the soul. He

Ram Mohan Roy.

was much influenced by Christianity and in 1820 published another book, *The Precepts of Jesus*. He became convinced that Hindu practices and forms of worship were corrupt, and wanted to bring about radical reform in Hinduism.

Ram Mohan Roy had studied Vedanta, Islam, Buddhism and Christianity, and he knew Bengali, Sanskrit, Pali, Persian, Arabic, Hebrew, Greek and English. He was well qualified to start his religious and social reform movement. He fought to abolish polytheism, polygamy, image worship, the caste system, child marriage, animal sacrifice and suttee. He advocated a wider system of public education through the medium of English, believing that the Sanskrit system of education only perpetuated ignorance. He came to England in 1830, when he spoke before the Select Committee of the House of Commons on Indian questions. Ram Mohan Roy died in Bristol in 1833 and was buried there.

Brahmo Samaj

In 1828 Ram Mohan Roy founded the Brahmo Samaj (Society of Brahma or God) in an attempt to bring about a radical transformation in Hindu life and religious practice. The *samaj* was meant to be a society of true worshippers of the One God of all religions, but in fact only Hindus joined. The hall of worship had no images, statues or pictures. Sacrifices and offerings to Agni, the God of Fire, were forbidden. Only prayers and hymns affirming One God were selected. Members gathered in the hall and offered worship as a group – this congregational form was new to Hinduism, in which worship had always been performed individually. In the *Bhakti* movement, ever since the Middle Ages, devotees had gathered in large numbers to sing devotional songs and to go on pilgrimages, but the actual worship was always offered to an image by each person individually, not as a group. The congregational form adopted by the Brahmo Samaj was based on the Christian way of worship, since the founder was inspired by Western ideas. This was perhaps the main reason why the *samaj* never gained popular appeal.

The movement did, however, provide a powerful inspiration for progressive movements in Hindu society, religion and politics. As a result of Ram Mohan Roy's work, Hindus began to question out-dated religious practices and made efforts to remove social injustices, which resulted in some important legislation:

- Lord William Bentinck's Regulation of 1829 prohibiting the burning of widows;
- The Abolition of Slavery Act, 1843;
- Caste Disabilities Removal Act, 1850;
- Hindu Widows' Remarriage Act, 1856;
- The Sarda Act prohibiting Child Marriage, 1929;
- Hindu Women's Right to Property Act, 1937;
- The Hindu Marriage Act, 1955;
- The abolition of untouchability in 1950;
- The extension under the Indian Constitution in 1950 of the right to vote to all adults.

All the above were the indirect result of the reform movement started by Ram Mohan Roy in 1828.

?

1   What factors inspired Ram Mohan Roy to found the Brahmo Samaj?
2   How were the services conducted in a Brahmo Samaj prayer hall? Why did the Brahmo Samaj fail to win popular support?

DAYANANDA (1824–83)

Dayananda was born in Kathiawar, Gujarat, into a rich family who were ardent worshippers of Shiva. He was invested with the sacred thread when he was eight years old. One day, three years later, he was keeping vigil in a Shiva temple on the night of Mahashivaratri when, in the dead of night, he observed that rats appeared from the holes in the walls and began to eat the sacrificial food offered to Shiva. A doubt arose in his mind about the deity's power. How could the All-Powerful God allow these unclean creatures to feast on the food offered to Him alone? Soon after this incident, his sister and uncle died, and this started him thinking about death and the next life. When his parents arranged his marriage, he left home.

From the age of 20 he discoursed with various holy men to widen his knowledge of the Vedas and philosophy, travelling widely in his search for knowledge. At Mathura he met a blind *swami* (holy man) called Virajananda, who taught him the Hindu scriptures for three years. By the end of 1863, Dayananda's study was completed. His teacher charged him with the duty of spreading the Vedic faith.

He now became known as Swami Dayananda Saraswati. He started travelling again, teaching a new Vedic philosophy and denouncing image worship. He began to use Hindi to reach the masses of people who did not know Sanskrit. He met the leaders of the Brahmo Samaj in Calcutta and later those of the Prarthana Samaj in Bombay in 1874, but, sensing differences of opinion between himself and others in the two associations, he decided to start his own organisation.

Arya Samaj

Thus it was that Dayananda founded the Arya Samaj (Society of Aryans) in Bombay in 1875. Its greatest success was in the Punjab, and Lahore soon became the society's headquarters. Dayananda laid down the objectives of the movement in his book *Satyartha Prakash (Truth Manifest)*, which he wrote in Hindi.

Dayananda claimed the Vedas to be eternal, infallible and a complete revelation of God, given to the world millions of years ago. For the revival of Vedic religion, he asked his followers to go 'back to the Vedas'. He fancifully claimed that India was the fountainhead of all culture, material and spiritual, that Sanskrit was the parent of all languages and that all other cultures and religions were based on Vedic revelation. He saw in the Vedas the roots of all scientific advances.

He accepted the doctrines of *karma* and rebirth of the soul in another body, but stated that the soul could not be lost in the absolute (*Brahman*). His aim was to remove some practices of popular Hinduism, and so he opposed image worship, polytheism, animal sacrifice, the *shraddha* ceremony, caste based on birth, untouchability, pilgrimages and ritual bathing. He condemned child marriage and the segregation of women, but he did not permit the remarriage of widows. He formed a society for the protection of cows, and introduced 'purification rites' to reconvert those Hindus who had been converted to Christianity or Islam.

Arya Samaj followers worship on Sundays, and read, preach and teach the Vedas. Initiation, the daily performance of *havan* (offerings to sacred fire) and the recital of the Gayatri hymn are important aspects of the *samaj*, but it is a democratic organisation without regular priests. A certain percentage of members' income is expected to be paid into the funds of the organisation and every member is required to practise austerity, truth and devotion to God.

1   What experiences convinced Dayananda that the practices of popular Hinduism did not represent the religion of the Vedas?
2   Name the practices in popular Hinduism which are opposed by Arya Samaj.

PRARTHANA SAMAJ

This Prayer Society was founded in Bombay in 1867 after Keshab Chandra Sen, a prominent leader of the Brahmo Samaj in Calcutta, had inspired the people by his speeches in 1865. Prarthana Samaj was an important offshoot of the Brahmo Samaj.

Initially, the society had four aims:
- to oppose the caste system;
- to introduce widow remarriage;

- to encourage women's education;
- to abolish child marriage.

More objectives were added later.

The members described themselves as protestant Hindus and did not altogether give up their normal Hindu practices. They claimed that the *samaj* was in true line with the long established tradition of Vishnu worship in Maharashtra made popular by poet-saints like Namadeva, Tukaram and Ramadasa.

Important Social Reformers

Among the prominent members of the Prarthana Samaj were Ramkrishna Gopal Bhandarkar (1837–1925), an orientalist of profound scholarship, and Mahadev Govind Ranadé (1842–1901), an educationist and a leading social reformer, who later became a judge of the Bombay High Court. Both these men exercised great influence on the progress of Indian social, political and religious reform. Other important social reformers of western India, who were closely associated with M.G. Ranadé, were Lokamanya Tilak (1856–1920), an ardent nationalist, Gopal Krishna Gokhalé (1866–1915), a moderate and constitutional politician, and Pandita Ramabai, the pioneer in the field of educational and social reform for women.

**DEVEN-
DRANATH
TAGORE
(1818–1905)**

Devendranath Tagore was influenced by the Western philosophy of Locke and Hume. He rejected the Vedas and the Vedanta philosophy, and joined the Brahmo Samaj in the hope of finding a true religion. He was shocked, however, to find that the story of Rama's incarnation was being preached in the *samaj* and that non-Brahmins were excluded from the congregation when the Vedas were recited. He strongly condemned these practices, and soon they were stopped.

He started a reformed religious society called the Universal Brahmo Samaj. Finding that religious reform did not have popular support, he then left the Brahmo Samaj altogether and retired to a retreat known as Shantiniketan (Abode of Peace), which later became a university under the guidance of his son, the famous poet Rabindranath Tagore.

**KESHAB
CHANDRA SEN
(1838–84)**

Keshab Chandra Sen was born into a wealthy and influential family in Calcutta. After his formal education, he joined the Brahmo Samaj in 1857 and worked with Devendranath Tagore for the advancement of the *samaj*. When he was in his early twenties he founded a fortnightly paper, the *Indian Mirror*, to spread his ideas for social, religious and political reform, and he opened new branches of the *samaj*.

Keshab Chandra Sen held that prayer and meditation were essential to a godly life. He incorporated some elements of Christianity, such as the doctrine of the Trinity and Baptism, into the Brahmo Samaj. He advocated widow remarriage, but rejected the entire Hindu philosophy and the sacred thread. He wanted social reform to be the main objective of the *samaj*, but on this point a difference arose between himself and Tagore. He left the original *samaj* and founded his 'Brahmo Samaj of India' to include people of all races and communities, based on the idea of the fatherhood of God and brotherhood of man. Its scriptures included texts from seven different religions. His preaching included such basic ethical concepts as truth, love and selflessness.

In 1870 Sen went to England and delivered many lectures in public halls. He returned to India with fresh ideas regarding education and women's emancipation, and devised a new ritual for a Brahmo marriage. In 1872 such marriages became legally valid.

Towards the end of his life, in 1881, he revived the old Vedic ritual of sacrifice, the *arati*, introduced the celebration of Durga Puja into the *samaj* and gave his approval to image worship. Gradually his influence declined, but he was respected by all sections of society until his death in 1884.

RAMAKRISHNA (1836–86)

Gadadhar Chattopadhyaya was born into a Brahmin family in Bengal, and as a young man he worked as a temple-priest in the Kali temple near Calcutta. He suffered from epilepsy and profound depression. When he was 25, he was married to a girl of five. After the marriage he went back to the temple and returned his 'wife' to her father's house. Even when the girl came of age, the couple never lived together as man and wife.

During his life he never handled money, which he considered to be an obstacle in the path of experiencing God. He regularly meditated before the Kali image and considered her as his mother and the mother of the universe; he learned yoga practices from a woman devotee of Kali. A monk learned in the Vedanta philosophy initiated him as a *sannyasin* and gave him a new name, Ramakrishna.

Ramakrishna often went into a trance during meditation, and claimed to have had visions of the Hindu deities Kali, Shiva, Rama and Krishna. He underwent religious discipline guided by a Muslim saint, learned the teachings of the Bible from a friend, and tested both the religions through meditation. He claimed to have experienced visions of the Prophet and of Jesus.

He concluded that all religions were true and that it was possible to experience God by following different paths. He preferred Hinduism and remained a Hindu. He held that books on theology and philosophy *taught* about God, but that intuition, love, faith and surrender were the only means of *realising* and *experiencing* God. He stressed that all religions were different paths to the same God, and that 'Jiva is Shiva' (all life is God).

Ramakrishna met the prominent Hindu reformers like Tagore, Dayananda and Sen, and it was Keshab Chandra Sen who made him known to the world. Many educated people became his disciples – Narendranath Dutta (see below) being the chief among them. His talks and parables were full of the ancient wisdom of India. He died at the age of 50 of throat cancer.

1   Describe the experiences which convinced Ramakrishna that all religions were true.
2   Give a brief account of Ramakrishna's views about God, books on theology, different religions and a sure way of experiencing God.

VIVEKANANDA (1863–1902)

Narendranath Dutta was born in Calcutta and graduated from the Christian Missionary College. He had a deep knowledge of Western philosophy and in his youth he was much influenced by the writings of Herbert Spencer and J.S. Mill. After meeting Keshab Chandra Sen he joined the Brahmo Samaj. His life-long conviction was that Man was the master of his own destiny and was able to achieve perfection by his own efforts. In 1882, he met Ramakrishna and soon became his disciple. He was given a new name and a title, and became known as Swami Vivekananda.

He devoted six years to meditation in a Himalayan retreat, and then travelled widely in western and southern India. After the death of Ramakrishna in 1886, he claimed to have had visions, and, after deep study, he showed great ability in expounding Vedanta philosophy.

In 1893, Vivekananda was sent by the Raja of Ramnad to represent Hinduism at the Parliament of Religions in Chicago. He took the eastern route, stopping and lecturing at Singapore, Hong Kong, Tokyo and Vancouver, before finally reaching Chicago. Other delegates were impressed by his advocacy of Hinduism, which he presented as an idealised version of the faith, adjusted to suit American sentiments. His oratory at Chicago earned him international fame.

Swami Vivekananda.

He visited Britain and lectured on Vedanta philosophy. Margaret Noble became his disciple and later wrote her book, *The Web of Indian Life*, under her new name, Sister Nivedita. On his second visit to America, he founded the Vedanta Society of San Francisco, established Ramakrishna missions in other countries, and, after returning to India in 1897, he established his monastery near Calcutta. Until his death in 1902 he travelled widely in India, spreading his teachings of reformed Hinduism.

Social and Religious Beliefs

Vivekananda stressed the universal nature of Vedanta religion, and although he accepted all faiths as true, he declared that Hinduism was the mother of all religions. He supported image worship and held that there was no polytheism in Hinduism, since all Hindus believed in the existence of One Divine Power behind all images.

He opposed child marriage, Brahmin oppression of the lower castes, and the backward condition of women, and held that 'Service to Mankind' was the best religion in the world. He admired American materialism and advocated that it should be coupled with Vedanta philosophy in India. He wanted to see material prosperity in India, so that a kind of vigorous Hinduism might develop. He held that physical strength and spiritual fearlessness were essential to the understanding of *atman* and the Bhagavad-Gita, and he proclaimed non-violence to be moral and intellectual suicide.

Although he disapproved of the conversion of Hindus to Christianity, the work of the Ramakrishna missions all over the world is carried out along Christian missionary lines, involving educational, social and spiritual activities.

?

1 Explain how Vivekananda was influenced by Western and Eastern philosophy.
2 Did Vivekananda accept that fatalism was usually associated with the doctrine of *karma*? Did he reject Western materialism?
3 Describe briefly the views put forward by Vivekananda in relation to Vedanta, the caste system and non-violence.

MAHATMA GANDHI (1869–1948)

Born Mohandas Karamchand, the title Mahatma (Great Soul) was conferred on Gandhi by Rabindranath Tagore in 1914 when he returned to India from South Africa. He was born on 2 October 1869, son of the Prime Minister of Porbandar, a princely state in Gujarat. His parents were worshippers of Vishnu. Gandhi was married to Kasturba when they were both 13. When he was 15, his father was very ill and on the point of death. Gandhi was in the next room with his wife when his father died, and he felt a deep and lasting guilt for having deserted his father at the moment of death; this experience influenced him throughout his later life.

Gandhi was sent to England, where he studied law; on his return to India, he practised as a lawyer for some time. Then for 20 years, between 1893 and 1914, he worked as a lawyer in South Africa; it was here, when he was fighting for the rights of Indians who had settled in South Africa, that he first put to the test his theory of *Satyagraha* (insistence upon truth) as a political weapon.

Gandhi was born into a devout family and grew up with the *varna-ashrama-dharma* philosophy. He accepted the caste system, but opposed the privileges which high-caste Hindus claimed because of their position in the hierarchy. He fell victim to the practice of child marriage, and strongly opposed it when he realised its dangers. His inflexible opposition to untouchability provided him with an objective: to fight social injustice in Hindu society. As a high-caste Hindu he boldly undertook to do the dirty job of cleaning latrines (toilets), which the untouchables were condemned to do all their lives. By doing this work he set an example to his followers; he also wanted to find out what it felt like to be an untouchable. He gave them a new name, Harijans, meaning 'Children of God', but this did not improve their condition during his lifetime. It was not until 1950 that the law finally took notice of his lifelong work, but all that was abolished was the practice of untouchability, not the caste system.

Religious Beliefs

Western education, a long stay in a foreign country where the colour of one's skin was more important than ability, and the study of the New Testament, all helped to make Gandhi more aware of his Hindu religion. His ideals were *dharma* (duty), *satya* (truth), *ahimsa* (non-violence) and *moksha* (spiritual liberation). His lifelong search for Truth, which he equated to God or Ultimate Reality, was coupled with non-violence when he formed his idea of *Satyagraha* (literally, 'Truth Force'). Truth was the end or objective; non-violence was the means to gain that objective. Gandhi used religious principles in his politics, the aim of which was to get rid of the British from India, when he joined the Indian National Congress in 1915.

In addition to the New Testament, Gandhi gained inspiration from and found solace in the teachings of the Bhagavad-Gita. Its central teaching is about *varna* duty, even if that duty involves killing an enemy. It also explains the nature of *atman, Brahman*, the material world with the three *gunas*, and recommends the paths of selfless action, knowledge, yoga and devotion to achieve spiritual liberation. How could Gandhi, a pacifist, gain inspiration from the Gita, in which Krishna's central advice to Arjuna was: 'Throw off your doubts and fight, for it is your duty as a Kshatriya'? This was totally against Gandhi's philosophy of non-violence.

Gandhi put forward this interpretation: Krishna's advice to Arjuna implied that Arjuna's fight was a spiritual conflict only; Krishna was speaking of the conflict between good and evil which every person experiences. According to Gandhi, the central teaching of the Bhagavad-Gita is *anasakti* (non-attachment) and *nishkama karma* (selfless action); non-violence is included in non-attachment.

The Gita does, of course, include many other concepts apart from selfless action. Gandhi's interpretation was similar to many earlier interpretations which were made to prove sectarian viewpoints. Even so, there is no doubt that Gandhi was one of the best in putting selfless action into practice.

Satyagraha

Satyagraha is a religious technique which can be interpreted as 'insistence on truth and non-violent acceptance of the consequences'. Gandhi said he learned it from Kasturba, his wife, and he used it to bring about social and political change. The four essentially religious elements, which make a true follower of *Satyagraha*, are: truth; non-violence; self-control; and penance or sacrifice.

Earlier experiments with the 'Truth Force' were only partially successful and had resulted in violence. The most effective *Satyagraha* was launched in April 1930, as a protest against the Indian government's salt monopoly. Gandhi argued that salt was essential to the poor, since they could not afford any spices, and that people should be able to make their own salt from sea water. He gave notice of the protest to the Viceroy and, starting from his ashram at Sabarmati, he walked to Dandi on the west coast of India. In a symbolic gesture, he picked up a pinch of salt from the beach, thereby breaking the law. The picture on page 56 shows him and his followers just after this Salt March. A month later he was arrested. Even when he was in jail, his followers continued the *Satyagraha* and suffered beatings with long sticks by the Indian police. The British authorities in India considered Gandhi's activities as a political nuisance, but to Gandhi they were religious acts in his 'experiment with truth'. At the start of the march to Dandi, he and his followers had sung a hymn in praise of Rama.

?

1 How and where did Gandhi test his theory of *Satyagraha*?
2 Did Gandhi totally reject the caste system? What were his religious ideals?
3 Describe briefly Gandhi's 'salt-*satyagraha*' in April 1930 and say whether, in your opinion, it was political or religious in character.

AUROBINDO (GHOSH) (1872–1950)

Sri Aurobindo (Ghosh) was born into a rich family in Calcutta and, after a primary education at a European convent in India, he was sent to England at the age of seven. His English education lasted for 14 years. He obtained a degree in classics at Cambridge University and passed the Indian Civil Service examination. He was disqualified

Sri Aurobindo.

from entering the Civil Service, however, because he failed the riding test at the end of his two years' probation.

On his return to India, he was appointed Vice-Principal of Baroda College, where he learned Sanskrit. In 1902 he joined the national struggle for self-government, advocated the use of Indian goods, and started two journals, *Bande Mataram* and *Karma Yogin*. He was imprisoned by the British in 1908 and, while in prison for one year, he studied yoga. In 1910, he avoided further prosecution by escaping to the French controlled area of Pondicherry in India. Here he started an ashram where he could teach yoga and Hindu philosophy. After his long education in the West, Aurobindo went back to his Hindu roots and evolved a complex philosophy based on the practice of yoga, which he regarded as essential for the ideas of the new age.

Aurobindo's Philosophy

His central belief was that dynamic *shakti* manifests itself as energy and matter, but that the latter is shaped by the former. This *shakti* principle is often equated to *Brahman*, since *Brahman* is the Sole Reality behind all things, creatures and actions in the universe. Below *Brahman* there are several planes of existence, acting and reacting one upon the other. From *Brahman* flows *satya* (truth), *chit* (wisdom), and *ananda* (bliss). On the lowest plane are mind, life and matter. The dormant spirit in matter rises towards the Divine.

According to Aurobindo's theory, the descent of *Brahman* and the ascent of the individual spirit merge through *Purna Yoga*, or Integral Yoga. This form of yoga concentrates the divine energy, which is split up throughout creation, turning it once more into a divine force. Aurobindo wanted the salvation of the entire human race; his Integral Yoga requires complete surrender to God, which alone frees man from egoism and leads to ultimate bliss. Aurobindo developed his philosophy over a period of 40 years and he wrote many books on it.

1   Where was Sri Aurobindo educated? Under what circumstances did he study yoga?
2   Give a brief account of Aurobindo's central belief.
3   For what purpose did Aurobindo advocate his theory of Integral Yoga?

<table>
<tr><td>

Chapter

17

</td><td>

Dialogue with other Faiths

</td></tr>
</table>

HINDUISM IN BRITAIN

Figures quoted in *Hinduism in Great Britain*[1] show there were approximately 307 000 Hindus in Britain in 1977. Of this number, 70 per cent were Gujarati in origin, 15 per cent Punjabi, and the remaining 15 per cent came either from other regions of India such as Bengal, Tamil Nadu, Maharashtra, Bihar and Uttar Pradesh, or from Sri Lanka. More recent figures tell us that there are now about 350 000 Hindus in Britain.[2]

Many children in British schools today are British by birth but Hindu by religion, because of their parents' faith. The presence of Hindu children in a school gives an opportunity to non-Hindu pupils to find out through conversation about aspects of Hindu religious experience.

Exploring Hinduism in room.

SECTARIAN HINDUISM AND INTER-FAITH DIALOGUE

The Hinduism practised by a large majority of Hindus in Britain is sectarian in character and does not give a full picture of the faith. Even though the sects are part and parcel of the wider Hindu tradition, the practice of the followers of, for example, the Swaminarayan religion, the Sathya Sai Baba movement and the Hare Krishna religion, present a partial and narrow view of Hinduism. The followers of these faiths tend to insist that theirs is the only correct way, a view which goes against the general tolerance in matters of doctrine which is the important characteristic of the wider Hindu tradition, the *Sanatana-dharma*, or universal law.

Hinduism does not attempt conversion into its fold; the practice of 'conversion' advocated by the Arya Samaj (see Chapter 16) has always been limited to the 'reconversion' of former Hindus who were tricked or forced into other faiths.

 Why don't Hindus try to convert other people to their beliefs?

Although Hindus have complete freedom in matters of belief, the various texts and manuals have established considerable uniformity of practice, and, in spite of regional and local variations, the performance of many rituals and sacraments is fairly uniform among Hindus. This is reflected in the *mantras* for the sacred thread ceremony, marriage and cremation, which have not altered for nearly 2000 years.

The same cannot be said for belief, since Hindus are free to worship the Supreme Spirit as represented in the Vishnu, Shiva or Shakti traditions. This freedom of worship creates a self-contained religious insularity, and has led to the 'live-and-let-live', 'separate-but-equal' attitudes of Hindus towards the different sects within Hinduism as well as towards other faiths. Hindus will not deny the validity of another religion, but they will not feel any need to find out about it either.

A person has to possess sufficient curiosity about another's faith before a meaningful exchange of ideas can take place. Because of the factors mentioned earlier, most Hindus tend to lack curiosity about belief and patterns of worship in other religions and are rarely interested in holding a dialogue with the followers of other faiths.

There is great diversity in Hinduism, but are there any beliefs and/or practices which most Hindus seem to agree to be important? Make a list of any you can think of.

BARRIERS TO INTER-FAITH DIALOGUE

The practical demonstration of faith is all-important to Hindus, who maintain that their faith depends upon it. They are particularly careful about food, spiritual purity, and entering the place of worship of another faith, such as a church or a mosque. This was one of the reasons why thousands of Hindus once felt that they had lost their faith after drinking water from a village well which had been 'polluted' by the Portuguese Christians, who had thrown bread into it. Very few, if any, Hindus will be able to distinguish between different churches or to describe from first-hand experience the services held on Sundays, even after a life-time in Britain. They are not against other faiths; they simply feel that they do not need to know how non-Hindus worship God.

The historical memory of forced conversions of Hindus to Islam or to Christianity in India has a subconscious influence on the Hindu mind, and this makes it difficult to establish an open dialogue with other faiths.

ACHIEVE-MENTS IN INTER-FAITH DIALOGUE

The outlook is not entirely negative, however, because the attitudes of many Hindu community leaders, of officials at some Hindu temples, of some Hindu writers and of many individual Hindus, are gradually changing. People are beginning to see the need for understanding their neighbour's faith, and are taking part in inter-faith meetings and discussions.

Christian churches in Britain have begun several initiatives which have had considerable success in inter-faith dialogue; there have been marches, shared worship, celebrations of the major festivals of all faiths, discussion groups and lectures. Hindus have shared in these, although they are always only a minority of the participants. The events are usually locally, rather than nationally, based, but this may be an advantage, since small but enthusiastic groups, whose members know each other well and who can work together with community relevance, may achieve more in the long run than large, 'one-off' gatherings addressed by well-known speakers who leave after the event, with no further contact with the participants.

A handful of Hindus in recent years have been writing about Hinduism in order to explain their faith to others, but with no intention on their part to convert others to Hinduism. To proselytise, to convert, is not the way of the *Sanatana-dharma*, although some modern Hindu sects have broken this tradition.

INTER-FAITH ORGANISATIONS IN BRITAIN

The Inter-Faith Network for the United Kingdom (5–7 Tavistock Place, London WC1H 9SS, tel: 01–388 0008) is the central organisation which provides the link between a number of national representative and inter-faith organisations, local inter-faith groups, study centres and educational bodies. It is not a policy-making body, but it provides a forum for dialogue between members of different religious traditions, encourages the work of local inter-faith groups, and gives guidance and information on inter-faith matters to the wider public. The Network's handbook lists names and addresses of various affiliated organisations. There are 21 national representative organisations, 6 national inter-faith organisations, 28 local inter-faith groups and 10 study centres and educational bodies.

The following organisations, representing some aspects of wider Hinduism, are active in inter-faith work:

- Arya Pratinidhi Sabha (UK)
  69A Argyle Road, West Ealing, London W13
- National Council of Hindu Temples
  559 St Alban's Road, Watford, Herts WD2 6JH
- Swaminarayan Hindu Mission, Inter-Faith Committee
  14 Michleham Down, Woodside Park, London N12 7JN
- Vishwa Hindu Parishad (UK)
  5 Rosemary Drive, Redbridge, Ilford, Essex IG4 5JD

Many individual Hindus take part in the work of local inter-faith groups, which helps to promote better understanding of the Hindu tradition through personal contact.

1   Make a collection of Indian stamps related to places, people and aspects of Hinduism that you have learned about in this book. Mount them as an exhibition, with explanatory captions.

2   Prepare a ten-minute talk to give to your parents or to a governor, or even to a Hindu visitor, telling them what you think is the 'essence' of Hinduism.

3   Now that you have studied Hinduism, what do you think the word 'religion' means?

4   Some people say there is no such thing as Christianity, Hinduism, etc., there are only Hindus, Christians, etc. What do you think they mean? From your studies, what arguments can you put forward to support and dispute this view?

Notes

1   R. Burghart (ed.), *Hinduism in Great Britain* (Tavistock Publications, 1987), page 8.

2   Research paper by Dr Kim Knott, Department of Theology and Religious Studies, University of Leeds, printed in 'Sikh Bulletin' No. 4, 1987, page 19.

Further Reading

TEACHERS' BOOKS

David Bowen, (ed.), *Hinduism in England* (Bradford College, 1981)
R. Burghart, (ed.), *Hinduism in Great Britain* (Tavistock Press, 1987)
W. Owen Cole, *Six Religions in the Twentieth Century* (Hulton, 1985)
R. Jackson (ed.), *Perspectives on World Religions* (SOAS, 1978)
Helen A. Kanitkar and R. Jackson, *Hindus in Britain* (SOAS, 1982)
V.P. (Hemant) Kanitkar, *Hindu Festivals and Sacraments* (The author, 1984)
    (Available from V.P. Kanitkar, 83 Bulwer Road, New Barnet, Herts. £5 incl. p.&p.)
V.P. (Hemant) Kanitkar, *We are Hindus* (The St Andrew Press, 1987)
D. Killingley and R. Jackson, *Approaches to Hinduism* (John Murray, 1988)
K. Knott, *Hinduism in Leeds* (University of Leeds, 1986)
John M. Koller, *The Indian Way* (Macmillan, 1982)
Wendy O'Flaherty, *Hindu Myths* (Penguin Classics, 1987)
S. Radhakrishnan and C. Moore, (eds.), *A Sourcebook of Indian Philosophy* (Princeton University Press, 1973)
C. Shackle, (ed.), *South Asian Languages: A Handbook* (SOAS, 1985)
Ninian Smart, *Hindu Patterns of Liberation*, Units 6, 7 and 8 (The Open University, 1981)
Simon Weightman, 'Hinduism' in J. Hinnells, (ed.), *A Handbook of Living Religions* (Penguin, 1984)
Simon Weightman, *Hinduism in a Village Setting* (The Open University, 1978)
Raymond Williams, *A New Face of Hinduism: The Swaminarayan Religion* (Cambridge University Press, 1984)
Angela Wood (ed.), *Religions and Education*, Sections 12–16 (BFSS National RE Centre, West London Institute of Higher Education, 1989)
R.C. Zaehner, *Hindu Scriptures* (J.M. Dent, 1966)

PUPILS' BOOKS

Patricia Bahree, *The Hindu World* (Macdonald Educational, 1982)
Patricia Bahree, *A Dictionary of Hinduism* (Batsford, 1984)
John Baily, *Religious Leaders and Places of Pilgrimage Today* (Schofield and Sims, 1987)
W. Owen Cole, *Meeting Hinduism* (Longman, 1987)
Jamila Gavin, *Stories from the Hindu World*, (Macdonald, 1986)
R. Jackson, *Religions through Festivals (Hinduism)* (Longman, 1988)
V.P. (Hemant) Kanitkar, *Hindu Stories* (Wayland, 1986)
Sauresh Ray, *Saraswati Puja* (RMEP, 1985)
Elizabeth Seeger, *The Five Sons of King Pandu* (J.M. Dent, 1970)
Brian Thompson, *The Story of Prince Rama* (Kestrel Books, 1980)
Swami Yogeshananda, *The Way of the Hindu* (Hulton, 1973)

Glossary

Agni	the Lord of Fire
Akara	shape or form
Antarala	the space between the assembly hall and the inner shrine in a temple
Ardha-Mandap	a porch at the front of a temple
Artha	one of the four aims of life
Arya	noble
Asceticism	the practice of rigorous self-discipline, fasting, meditation and prayer
Ashrama	a stage in life, e.g. student stage, householder stage, etc.
Atharva-Veda	the fourth Veda
Atman	the animating energy in any living creature, usually referred to as the Soul
Aum	the sacred syllable (also spelt Om) – it is believed to contain the sound of all Reality
Avatar	an incarnation of God (The *avatars* of Vishnu are more widely worshipped than those of Shiva.)
Bhagavad-Gita	an important and popular Hindu religious book
Brahmacharya	the student stage in life
Brahman	the Supreme Spirit in Hinduism
Brahmanas	religious texts composed for the guidance of priests in the performance of sacrifices
Brahma	the Creator aspect of *Brahman* in the Hindu *Trimurti*
Brahma-Sutras	holy books in concise verse containing Hindu philosophy
Brahmin	a member of the first group in the social divisions called *varna*
Caste	an occupational group within the larger *varna* divisions
Darshan	viewing an image in a temple
Deity	a name for a God or a Goddess
Deva	a Sanskrit word for God
Devata	a minor deity
Devi	a Sanskrit word for Goddess
Dharma	religious or moral duty of a Hindu based on his/her age, education, occupation and social position
Dharma-Shastra	a book containing the customary law relating to social conduct
Dhoti	a cotton garment, five metres long and one metre wide, worn to cover the lower part of the body
Ganga	Indian name for the river Ganges
Garbha-Griha	the innermost room in a Hindu temple where the image of a deity is installed, the holiest part of a temple
Gayatri	a hymn from the Rig-Veda praising the Sun God
Gopuram	the tallest structure above the main gateway in a south Indian temple
Grihastha	a householder; the second stage in life
Havan	a sacrifice where offerings are made to the sacred fire
Indus	a holy river whose Hindu name is *Sindhu*
Ishta-Devata	a personal deity worshipped by a Hindu (see *Ishwara*)
Ishwara	a personal deity worshipped by a Hindu
Jati	Indian word for caste, signifying one's social position, which is determined by occupation
Jnana	philosophical knowledge of God, man and man's position in the world
Kama	enjoyment of the good things in life; the third aim in life

Karma	the total effect of one's actions (The word also means action.)
Kshatriya	a member of the second group in the *varna* division
Kum-Kum	red powder used in a *puja*; it is also used as a *tilak* on the forehead
Mandala	a religious diagram used in a special *puja* or meditation
Mandap	the assembly hall in a temple
Mangala Sootra	the marriage necklace of a Hindu woman
Mantra	a sacred formula, always in Sanskrit
Moksha	liberation of the soul from successive births and deaths
Murti	an image of a deity in a temple
Namaskar	Indian word for greeting
Om	the sacred syllable (see *Aum*)
Pinda	a ball of cooked rice offered to the spirits of departed ancestors at the time of *shraddha*
Prasad	a blessed offering distributed among the worshippers at the end of a *puja*
Puja	a common form of Hindu worship
Puranas	ancient Hindu myths and legends
Rig-Veda	the first of the four ancient holy books
Sacred thread	a loop of three or five strands of strong cotton thread used in the initiation ceremony
Sama-Veda	the third Veda, an ancient holy book
Samsara	the cycle of successive births, deaths and rebirths
Samskara	a life-cycle ritual performed at important stages during a person's life, to purify the body and the spirit
Sanatana-dharma	the ancient or eternal way of life
Sannyasi	a person who gives up his name, family ties and most of his possessions, and devotes his life to meditation in order to attain liberation (*moksha*)
Sanskrit	an ancient language of India
Satya	truth
Satyagraha	'the insistence upon truth', a method of non-cooperation used by Mahatma Gandhi
Shikhara	the tallest structure above the image in a north Indian temple
Shraddha	the annual rites of offering *pinda* to the spirits of the deceased ancestors. (The first 'a' is sounded as 'a' in *car*.)
Shruti	a holy book believed to have been 'revealed' by God to wise men, and therefore 'heard' by them
Shudra	an artisan, a member of the fourth group in the *varna* division
Smriti	a holy book, composed by wise men from 'remembered tradition'
Upanishad	a book of Hindu philosophy
Vaishya	a member of the third group in the *varna* division
Vanaprastha	the retirement stage in life
Varna	a social category (The four *varnas* are Brahmin, Kshatriya, Vaishya and Shudra.)
Vedanta	a system of philosophy composed at the end of the Vedic period
Vimana	the inner sanctuary in a temple (see *Garbha-Griha*)
Yajur-Veda	the second Veda; an ancient holy book of the Aryans concerned with the performance of sacrifice
Yama	the Spirit of Death
Yamuna	a holy river in north India, also spelt *Jumna*
Yatra	a pilgrimage; the word also means a procession
Yoga	a system of philosophy combining physical exercises and meditation

Index

Note: **bold** numbers indicate pages where the main explanation of a word is given.